Also by William Pillow
Grave Convictions
Love and Immortality: Long Journey of My Heart

MEET YOURSELF AGAIN

for the

FIRST TIME

Hidden Forces Shape Our Lives

WILLIAM PILLOW

iUniverse, Inc.
New York Bloomington

Meet Yourself Again for the First Time
Hidden Forces Shape Our Lives

Copyright © 2009 William Pillow

iUniverse books may be ordered through booksellers or by contacting:

iUniverse
1663 Liberty Drive
Bloomington, IN 47403
www.iuniverse.com
1-800-Authors (1-800-288-4677)

ISBN: 978-1-4401-2672-7 (pbk)
ISBN: 978-1-4401-2673-4 (ebk)

Library of Congress Control Number: 2009902506

Printed in the United States of America

iUniverse rev. date: 6/4/2009

For my loving family

Contents

Acknowledgments

Our Creator and my family naturally come first for my gratitude in being able to write this book. But two other persons have served unceasingly in mentoring my writing, both from differing points of expertise. A third person kindly helped substantiate my research.

Lillian Stover Wells, PhD, retired dean of psychology at National University, has been of unparalleled assistance with regard to concepts in the book. Jack McMahan, a student of science and religion with degrees in theology and philosophy, continues to oversee grammatical and philosophical aspects of the book. Christian Felder, PhD, a neuroscientist, graciously reviewed and helped expand the section on "The Dynamic Brain."

I also am indebted to Joseph Chilton Pearce for his seminal book *The Biology of Transcendence: A Blueprint of the Human Spirit* (2002). It helped me integrate the conscious and unconscious minds with what some researchers term the "superconscious mind." To me, this connection seems to be the goal of ultimate transcendence.

PREFACE

IN THIS HIGH-TECH AGE, SOME computer scientists have predicted that robots might eventually be programmed to think and act like people. This may sound like science fiction. But suppose you and I and everyone else already have been programmed for certain parts of our behavior … without our realizing it? This concept surfaced in my research expanding upon a topic in my previous book, *Love and Immortality: Long Journey of My Heart* (2008). That subject was fetal and newborn memories. I began to wonder how pervasively, if at all, these memories might influence our lives. With the encouraging assistance of several professionals who spent countless hours guiding my efforts, this book took shape.

I was educated and practiced as a pharmacist. I also worked for Eli Lilly and Company for thirty-four years. The last fifteen of those years were spent in continuing health professional education. I also have a master's in business education degree and lack only the thesis for a doctorate in business education. I taught business management at the college level, and I wrote several texts and articles on pharmacy continuing education and on interpersonal communications. I always was fascinated by human behavior, particularly as it reflects human nature. This book enables me to share with you new information that researchers are discovering about the human being, especially as it relates to human behavior and self-perception.

Neurobiologists and mental health professionals now acknowledge that each of us has two memory systems. "Explicit" memory is the one commonly called "memory." It begins around age two to three. "Implicit" memory, by contrast, begins in the womb and consists of subconsciously "imprinted" memories plus associated emotions. These are not consciously retrievable under ordinary circumstances. Yet they shape conditioned behavioral responses to internal and external stimuli throughout our lives, without our awareness.

What we're referring to are the nuances of human behavior and their natural causes. The word "natural" is used here to mean the impact of influences that surround each of us almost from the time of our conceptions. These influences are not identical for each of us; rather, they are highly individualized. Their sources are highly variable and include such things as: our parents and significant others, the environment in which we were reared, and the conditions we encountered growing up.

Most of us never have heard of implicit memory. Even if we had, we likely never recognized it as such a hidden, yet profoundly influential, part of us. Some parents with teenagers and grown children could very well feel that this book is an indictment of their parental responsibility if their offspring have problems. But how could any parents be blamed? Most believe they did their best and couldn't have known the pitfalls of implicit memory.

Mental illnesses are not necessarily attributable to impediments in these natural processes. However, advances in psychology and neurobiology promise new approaches that help us better understand and treat psychopathology more effectively. What you read in this book might help resolve lingering questions in your own life and better ensure the well-being of your off spring.

There seems to be an additional aspect of our creation that is pertinent to this book. This factor can have a significant social impact. It outlines the growth and development of the human brain from the fetal state forward. This is patterned along the evolutionary path nature established beginning with the primitive reptilian brain. We will trace this evolution as it became the template for our brains today. Thus we can identify where natural and societal changes over time can and did significantly alter natural intent. The potential outcome of such influences has been enormous. There is a growing interest in acknowledging and addressing these forces to offer promise for the future.

Consider, too, that for some of us, our early childhoods might have been characterized by "a disruption in a natural process." These disruptions may not result in a mental illness. Still, we can learn to be better prepared as a society to minimize or deal with such potential disruptions. This should strengthen our parenting and its lifelong impact on new generations of adults. This book therefore focuses on three perspectives: the mother or parents, the fetus or young child, and the self—as an older child, teenager, or adult.

The purpose of this book is to help us understand

- the complex individuals we are;

- the lifelong impact of events in our early years;

- our complicated, unpredictable society;

- our individual uniqueness as human beings;

- each human being's special nature and incomparable capabilities.

As the Christian apostle Paul said in his letter to the church at Corinth, "Now I see through the glass darkly, but then face to face. Now I know in part, but then shall I know even as I am known."

So, would you like to meet yourself again for the first time? This book is not intended to change you or even to suggest that you change yourself. Its sole purpose is self-revelation: learning what might make us behave as we do. With this realization, we might discover a personal path to a better life for us and for our offspring.

A wealth of scientific information on these topics is available from mental health professionals, both in published works and on the Internet. Many sources address multiple topics. Therefore, rather than cite individual references throughout this book, I have included a bibliography, which offers a variety of references. Often, these include Web site addresses. I have identified a few key sources from the bibliography in the text.

The bibliography lists authors and publications upon whose research this book is based, as well as events during which topics were discussed. More than one publication by the same author is cited in about a dozen instances. A parenthetical publication or copyright year is included in the text following these authors' names to differentiate between those sources. A single source is identifiable in the bibliography by the author names(s) and publication title shown in the text. In the absence of identifiable authors, I have listed references in the bibliography by title or source in alphabetical order. An index is provided also.

It is important to acknowledge that a few readers may object to the occasional mention of God, Creator, or similar terms. Humanity recognizes that the majority of people believe in a creative power beyond definition or comprehension. Some authors listed in the bibliography use such terms in their publications.

CHAPTER ONE

WHO ARE YOU?

EVERY DAY, MOST OF US are caught up in a maelstrom of events that often becomes routine. So we just carry out the actions, seldom pausing to reflect on them. Time has become very precious and our responsibilities often seem overwhelming. Getting everything done without a mishap may become our only goal. But it appears that some people are beginning to realize that this racetrack is circular. They question whether this is their true purpose in life. They begin to question the hallmarks of contemporary life:

- an insistent pursuit of power, wealth, or achievement—or even just survival
- a seemingly endless demand from others
- a need to be in multiple places at the same time
- a belated recognition of a missed or blundered opportunity

This book asks whether something in our human nature compels us to adhere to our rituals and routines. So many of us are caught up in these whirlwinds that we may wonder if we all are alike in this herd effect. Or are there natural forces shaping our behavior that we are unaware of? In a sense, this book asks, "Just how well do you *think* you know yourself?" After all, is your *self* only the sum total of your *conscious* attributes and shortcomings? As the Scottish poet Robert Burns lamented, "Oh, would some power the gift to give us, to see ourselves as others see us." Perhaps we could call this "meeting yourself again for the first time."

1

Reality

The jury is still out on exactly how all our body systems work together to create what we believe is reality. For example, I am consciously aware of what's happening around me when I'm awake. I have a mind that serves as a storehouse of information. I have a complex brain and an intricate system of nerves. But science is still grappling with the probability that consciousness, the mind, and the brain may be three separate entities. My reality may have subtle shades of difference from your reality. Even if we both see the same object, it can mean something different to each of us. For example, we are looking at your new car. For you, it's a dream come true, but it has a different meaning for me.

In our individual cultures, most of us believe that you and I are quite "normal." Our visible behavior usually complies with the expectations of the culture. However, these norms may differ widely. For example, compare street gangs with churchgoers, college professors with soccer moms, marathon runners with art collectors, and so forth. Our awareness of reality enables us to create a day-to-day perception of well-being. There are a few interruptions of awareness of individual violence somewhere. Security forces attempt to control erratic behavior that threatens life or limb. Still, lesser disputes punctuate our daily lives. Each of us holds to certain individual beliefs and expectations, and these occasionally conflict with one another. Since we can't read one another's minds, we must impute each other's motives and expectations. It does no good to ask intentions, because unvarnished truth is a rare commodity.

Historically, society has used various methods to deal with persons who were considered irretrievably beyond cultural bounds of acceptable behavior or beliefs. The Catholic Inquisition was an extreme example. Later centuries found numbers of people with misunderstood illnesses confined to mental hospitals. Fundamentalist religious beliefs among Muslims, Amish, and even Christians have imposed sanctions ranging from shunning to killing. Author Jon Krakauer stressed this in his book *Under the Banner of Heaven: A Story of Violent Faith*. But social behavior and commerce generally flow relatively unimpeded. Humankind seems to have come to expect all of these threatening influences as part of today's reality. This book does not to judge the system as much as it sheds light on how natural forces brought us to this state of existence.

As many readers recognize, comedian Bill Cosby has been a staunch advocate for better parenting. His and Alvin Poussaint's book *Come on People: On the Path from Victims to Victors* speaks to the African-American community. Yet its forcefulness and lessons speak to all Americans. Undeniable forces at work in our society have shaped the deterioration of a segment of our American family structure. Apparently, similar influences are redesigning family status around the globe. The ultimate impact of this could occur after it is too late to alter its path. Most of us may recognize these changes. As individual mothers or fathers, however, we may believe that the solution is beyond our individual abilities to achieve. Cultural attitudes often block the way. In many instances, also, economic survival preempts more personalized childcare. Unfortunately, we may cave in to environmental pressures with resignation.

Do You Really Know Yourself?

How far back into your childhood can you consciously remember? You may recall how you felt, the reason, and even the particular happening. Most people can't go back farther than ages three or four. This ability is part of what is termed "explicit," "autobiographical," "declarative," or "episodic" memory. Examples include such things as fun at the state fair, disputes with others, and last night's dinner. This is what most of us mean when we talk about memory. But what you consciously recall from your explicit memory typically doesn't kick in until ages two to four at the earliest. The timing seems to depend on the child's development of verbal abilities, conscious self-awareness, and interaction with others.

To realize the full potential impact of the multiple forces that can affect human lives almost from the time of conception, let's start by examining human memory.

Chapter Two

Memory

Infantile Amnesia

Psychologists and neurobiologists long have grappled with the stage of human life from conception through early childhood. The general attitude has been that nothing significant occurred, or is remembered, from that period. The belief that most of us are unable to recall events from prenatal to early postnatal years led to the psychological term "infantile amnesia." Undoubtedly, psychologists were convinced that no memory exists from before a certain age. As strange as it may seem, however, patients undergoing hypnotic regression have demonstrated accurate recall of certain events that occurred while they still were in the womb. The term "infantile amnesia" has a long history. The description of infantile amnesia appeared in the writings of St. Augustine (353–430 AD) as discussed in Caputo and Scanlon's book *Augustine and Postmodernism*.

Today, it is known that there are two memory systems operating in our bodies. One, discussed earlier, is explicit memory. The other memory system is the "implicit memory." It is said to develop even as early as sometime in the womb. Its major difference from explicit memory is that implicit memory is unconsciously recorded. In a sense, it is "imprinted" like electronic recordings and associated with emotions. Moreover, implicit memory seldom, if ever, can be *intentionally* or *consciously* recalled later in life. Quite likely, many people might question the vast significance of prenatal experiences. But advances in human pathology research have revealed that even some adult illnesses may have their roots in the neonatal stage of life. These include cardiovascular diseases, obesity, and even cancer. This shows how experiences, not just genes, can significantly affect human life.

Implicit Memory

Few teenagers or adults ever realize the significant impact that their parents, other people, and their environment have had on them as babies. Most people would be shocked to know that babies, even fetuses, are capable of unconsciously recording memories. These memories often are emotionally charged. They can unconsciously and unintentionally influence things like self-esteem, motivation, relationships with others, and even our personal health.

The implicit memory system involves a person's experiences as a fetus, a newborn, and a very young child. It typically involves emotions that can result from feelings of abandonment, verbal or physical abuse, or even caregiver distress, whether from parents or others. Some researchers say that the most indelible "imprints" of implicit memories are the ones that were repetitious, traumatic, or belittling to a very young child. In sharp contrast, there may be memories of a parent's loving smile, the devoted attention of a caregiver, or warm reassurances in times of trouble.

An implicit memory is elicited or "primed" whenever we later encounter a circumstance, or stimulus, that reminds us of an earlier experience. This may happen at any time without our realizing it. It may have a positive or a negative emotion associated with it, typically the same emotion we felt at the time of the earlier experience. It can produce an automatic, unconscious, and unintentional behavioral response. Some people may be unwilling to acknowledge the reality of implicit memory. They may disavow manifesting any automatic behavioral responses to implicit memories. But science has demonstrated that events, or "imprints," do create implicit memories. These, with their associated emotions, can cause us to react a certain way without our being aware of it.

For example, you may have had a mysterious feeling without knowing its source. It seemed to come from out of nowhere, unrelated to what was happening at the time. You also may have had certain bodily sensations that seemed to make no sense. There may be times, too, when you seem to have some inexplicable difficulty relating to certain other persons or to given situations. There may be a remarkable experience of déjà vu, the feeling of having visited a particular place or having had an almost identical experience before.

The concept of unconscious implicit memory has received sparse attention by the news media. But two relatively recent scholarly texts document neuroscientific advances in consciousness. They are: *Strangers to Ourselves: Discovering the Adaptive Unconscious*, written by Timothy Wilson; and *The New Unconscious (Social Cognition and Social Neuroscience)*, edited by Ran R. Hassin, James S. Uleman, and John A Bargh.

There are several reasons you haven't heard more about implicit memory in the public news media:

- a lingering skepticism about the existence and influence of implicit memory
- an infrequent mention of implicit memory in professional publications
- researchers' uncertainty as to how to deal most effectively with implicit memory
- a virtual impossibility of characterizing an individual's implicit memory

The uncertainty about an individual's implicit memory is not whether it exists, but precisely what experiences and emotions it retains. We all are aware that traumatic experiences are stored somewhere. These may be consciously or explicitly repressed if recorded after the child's development of explicit memory. But what if negative experiences, both physical and psychological, happen before the explicit memory system develops? That's where implicit memory is involved. In 1890, in his *Principles of Psychology*, William James differentiated between "voluntary and involuntary" attention. The latter seems applicable to implicit memory.

Canadian psychologist Peter Graf and the U.S. psychologist Daniel L. Schacter introduced implicit memory in 1985 in an article in the *Journal of Experimental Psychology: Learning, Memory, and Cognition*. The study of implicit memory in psychology began in the early 1980s, but a proliferation of professional literature on the subject did not appear until the early twenty-first century.

Mental health professionals seem to have been only modestly successful in uncovering specific implicit response "programs" in their patients. Implicit Association Tests (IATs) have helped identify implicit attitudes regarding such traits as racial prejudice. IATs use word or picture association techniques, but the vast hidden composite each of us has in implicitly programmed emotional responses appears virtually off-limits, especially to ourselves. This seems exemplified in the variability that individuals exhibit when asked to compare their implicit and explicit self-esteem. It seems natural to inflate one's explicit self-esteem—this is our conscious dimension of self.

An often-repeated illustration of the potential impact of implicit memory involved an obstetrician. During delivery of several patients in turn, he made a shocking remark to nurses: "Don't pay much attention to that one. He may not even make it." Surprisingly, that baby developed into a driven and successful adult. That adult recalled the obstetrician's comment during hypnotic regression. His psychiatrist was trying to learn why the man lived such an aggressive life. It seemed almost as if this ambitious adult *unconsciously* was trying to prove the obstetrician wrong.

It is worth noting that persons undergoing hypnotic regression to their fetal or newborn states have reported learning some amazing facts. These included that they were in a troublesome environment, that they were unwelcome, or that their parents wanted a child of a different gender.

In referring to implicit memory, neurobiologists speak of the "encoding" of information. In other words, this is the seemingly inexplicable way in which we unconsciously record experiences and emotions from our earliest days of life. It is noteworthy to recognize that the process of forgetting apparently is more superficial than scientists once believed. It seems to apply only to explicit memory. Alzheimer's and aging have been shown to erode explicit memory but not implicit memory.

Procedural Memory

Implicit memory sometimes has been called "procedural." A good example of the latter is driving skills. Conditioned responses in learning to drive enable us to navigate an automobile while our thoughts may be on other things. But few of us as adults can consciously recall events in which we learned specific driving skills. There certainly are times we drive "automatically," without giving much or any conscious thought to what we're doing. Procedural memory obviously reminds me to stay a safe distance behind the car in front of me or to turn on car headlights after dark.

Members of groups, such as families, may share responsibilities by procedurally learning different tasks. Imagine a farm family with twelve children ranging from newborn to age twelve. Older ones may be responsible for helping cook or do laundry, the next older ones for milking cows, the next older ones for cleaning house, and so forth. Each will learn his or her job so well that it becomes as automatic as driving a car is for an average adult. But procedural memory is the result of consciously learned skills, despite the fact that we typically cannot recall later in life specific events involving that instruction.

Perhaps the most important part of the broader implicit memory is those experiences we *felt* at the time, but never again would normally recall. Many of these experiences were accompanied by emotions, positive or negative, which we also can't recall. The nature of the emotions and the experiences may be indelibly imprinted in our implicit memory. Even if we encounter anything reminiscent of those experiences later in life, our unconscious mind may direct our behavior—without our being aware of it! For this reason, much of psychotherapy involves what is termed a "corrected emotional experience."

With procedural memory, we likely were consciously aware of the learning event at the time we learned it. Also, procedural learning may extend longer into childhood. Consider that we first learned to ride a tricycle, then to ride a bicycle, then to drive a car. Both procedural and implicit memory can automatically control our behavior without our being aware of it. But the associated emotions of implicit memory, positive or negative, typically are not found in procedural memory.

Implicit memory usually involves interpersonal situations. It apparently is not necessary to encounter a repeat of the same situation to stimulate the memory and its associated emotion. Simply being faced with someone or something reminiscent of the earlier events seems sufficient. These conditioned response memories are thought to be composites of repeated early experiences rather than stemming from single events.

Implicit memories are not just animal instincts such as fear, fight, or flight. Instead, they involve the forces that moderate our behavior throughout our lives: our emotions. These began to be shaped even before we were born. Implicit memories are said to be definitive, emotional, and experienced passively in a specific context. These can surface unconsciously and unintentionally when we encounter a person, place, or situation reminiscent of the imprinted, emotionally charged experience.

An unusual case of a comatose man illustrates the fascinating extent to which even the implicit memory of a smell can have startling effects. Apparently, a particular smell was associated in the man's implicit memory with a particular trauma in his early childhood. When inadvertently exposed to this smell, even though he was comatose, the man went into a physiological anxiety state.

Implicit memory includes such things as attitudes, stereotypes, motivation, and self-esteem. For example, imagine that you are a hard, dedicated worker but always seem to be passed over for promotions. A natural tendency might be to play the "blame game." Part of this could involve blaming not just others but yourself too. You might even develop an inferiority complex. Regarding implicit stereotype memory, even before the 2008 presidential election, several Web sites had begun speculating whether implicit prejudices would affect Senator Obama's electability.

World opinion seems to be in a state of flux about Muslims. Few Americans seem to have had much, if any, personal association with members of this culture. Also, it appears unlikely that our ancestors did. Even though our ancestral sources of implicit prejudices don't include Muslims, the news media is filled with negative images of them. Thus, most of our stereotypes of that culture are not implicit but consciously formed.

This leads me to speculate that terrorist activity by militant Muslims and their clerical leaders might be designed to foster an unfavorable attitude toward the Muslim culture. In other words, Muslims' acceptance and assimilation into countries like America could become very emotionally charged. Is that the intent of theocratic Muslim leaders? Do they seek to rally support from even the more moderate and peace-loving Muslims, in an effort to justify an imposed theocracy as an individual defensive measure?

Explicit Memory

Autobiographical (explicit) memory is said to typically begin sometime during the third year of life, as children develop verbal and symbolic language skills. This facilitates cognition for describing themselves to others and, in doing so, remembering themselves. Explicit memories also can be associated with emotions, such as the time a parent caught a child smoking secretively and severely reprimanded him or her. The child likely will long remember the experience. Such a child may not have developed a sufficiently effective self-conscious evaluation system to reason whether the reprimand is justifiable. Nevertheless, that memory may influence his or her later behavior or attitude toward the parent.

But implicit memory begins even earlier, especially when a parent, a sibling, or a significant other berates a very young child. That child may be accused of being ugly, worthless, or dumb. He or she will not recall the experience but subconsciously will retain, and unquestionably believe, the judgment. Why not? It is from someone the child accepts as a supreme source of authority. Thus, this can manipulate his or her implicit self-esteem and future behavior without a conscious awareness. Extend this situation to a child who is criticized as sickly or weak—this actually could affect his or her immune system.

Research Advances

As mentioned, science used to believe that human beings have no memory of their experiences from the womb or first year or two of life. But hypnotic regression and electronic brain imaging contradict that assumption. Now science has demonstrated the potential error of ignoring these early stages of a child's life. David Hartman and Diane Zimberoff provided an excellent review of some of these advances in their article "Memory Access to Our Earliest Influences" in the *Journal of Heart-Centered Therapies*. Eventually, psychologists acknowledged that at least two distinct memory systems appear to operate in humans.

Researchers seem able to confirm this through the use of new functional brain scanning devices like MRIs. Implicit memory has been well established as separate from explicit memory. It seems promising that some mental health professionals now acknowledge that certain mental illnesses may be rooted in implicit memory. As you might imagine, our imprinted unconscious responses could create tensions with our conscious intended behavior.

How comfortable are you with learning that these unconscious imprints exist? You may have had a happy, reassuring start on life. You probably get along pretty well with other people. You likely have become accustomed to your circumstances. Would it interest you and possibly even help if you better understood your total *self*?

We all are subject to automatic responses programmed into us, beginning even before we left the womb. Our behavior can be affected, too, by implicit attitudes and beliefs about self, others, and the world around us. Suppose you could gain some insight to automatic behavioral responses programmed into you. Would it seem threatening? Or would you want to know yourself better? Conceivably, this might free you to improve your life: to access what has been called "free will." This is the supposed ability to make decisions and act without behavioral restraints imposed by automatic implicit responses.

One way to know yourself better might be hypnotic regression. On the other hand, with some personal research, you might learn certain historical facts surrounding your birth and early childhood. This could be supportive, as you recognize that lives change over time. Some of your implicit imprints may deserve reinforcing and others may fade in the light of day.

Impact of Implicit Memory

It seems reasonable that our implicit memory may be responsible for unusual feelings that each of us occasionally has had but didn't understand. These include subtle impulses, urges, and motivations. A minister once expressed to me his concern about how we might distinguish between talking with God and talking with our inner demons. No doubt he meant the ubiquitous influence that our emotions, fears, anxieties, urges, and drives have on our behavior. Some of these obviously are explicit—we are fully aware of them. But the implicit ones are not so recognizable.

For example, marketing efforts often are designed to appeal to our instinctual, implicit, or subliminal responses. But they also may try to motivate us toward a particular brand based upon our conscious appraisal of the product: taste, feel, quality of viewing or sound, or smell. However, because impulses, urges, and motivations in the implicit mind can vary substantially from person to person, marketing ploys may find some people responding negatively to certain product promotions.

Perhaps the most likely expressions of implicit memory occur in interpersonal relations, when another person's action "strikes a chord" in us. Then, we may respond impulsively—without even the foggiest idea why. This usually goes unnoticed by bystanders as anything other than evidence of one's personality. However, if this behavior becomes frequent, beyond one's control, and far outside societal norms, psychopathology might be suspected. In sharp contrast to urges, impulses, and motivations that can emerge unintentionally, we may harbor certain inhibitions in our implicit memory. A fear of heights, an aversion to certain foods, and a reluctance to be alone are only three examples.

There is no surefire way to solve the dilemma of being unconsciously influenced by implicit memory. Psychotherapy has introduced a variety of approaches intended to address the impact of implicit memory, but apparently with varying results. The new concept of neuroplasticity appears promising, assuring us that the wiring in our brains can be influenced to change. This offers hope, since it apparently can be achieved without regard to our age. Neuroplasticity is discussed in a later chapter.

From Generation to Generation

However undesirable our implicit programming may seem to be, it has a natural purpose: to prepare us for living and coping in our *natural* parents' setting. This introduces another realization. Given that we acquired our early emotions and conditioned responses (implicit memory) unconsciously from our parents, is there any doubt that our grandparents, in turn, had similarly "programmed" our parents? In other words, were some of the influences our parents had on us not original with them, but carried over from their parents?

Consider this example. Families in the Victorian era were very protective of both their young and their image. Forbid that a child be born out of wedlock. The term "illegitimate" was a common stigma, for the child, for the mother, and for her family. The family would go to any lengths to avoid having such a disgrace known. Years ago, chaperones were required to accompany young, unmarried women in public. Even today, in some Middle Eastern countries, a girl may be punished for being caught alone with a male who is not a family member. In the United States, parents began permitting their daughters to go on dates provided that a second couple joined them. Apparently, these parents found some reassurance that their daughter might not misbehave in the presence of the second couple.

Remnants of this prohibition existed in the behavior of some parents during the mid-twentieth century, especially those who jealously guarded their social standing. But the situation today may illustrate a change of permissiveness. Even explicit restrictions seem susceptible to modifications under the barrage from peer and public influences. This is notably exemplified as a product of the behavior of young "role models" in the entertainment industry. One might wonder whether parental influence succumbed to a variety of modern societal pressures. Examples include disruptions in the family unit, authority challenges from young people, or a general lethargy toward illegitimacy among the populace. Any existing fragile relations within a family risk tilting teenagers' behavior toward peer influence. Both implicit and explicit "instructions" have a powerful foe in an adolescent child with unbridled independence.

Some parents remained very protective of their daughters, displaying suspicion about boys and even refusing to allow them much choice in their leisure activities. As a result, immature adolescents often seemed to manifest an open hostility toward their parents. This had the potential of spreading to other relationships between children and their parents. The young may have openly challenged their parents' authority. Why else would some teenagers display risky behavior and associate with persons of questionable reputation?

However, it must be acknowledged that certain families are able to establish and maintain honest, open relationships with their children.

Even today, certain teenagers on their own display remarkably mature decision making to avoid compromising situations. In her lectures at the University of Wisconsin, Marlowe Embree introduced the concept that parents have a "filtering device" that helps control their implicit imprints on their children.

But consider the following example: Margaret was an aloof mother to Janet, a trait she received and passed on from her own Victorian mother. "Children are to be seen, not heard!" was the motto Margaret never questioned. Janet therefore found it difficult to relate to her mother, and this impression was imprinted into her implicit memory. Apparently, Janet accepted that this is how mothers are and ought to be. Guess what Janet's relationship was with her children?

Also: Sean was an Irish bartender. He ruled the roost at home. Frequently coming home late and beating up his wife, he also would abuse his kids the following morning. A dutiful Irish wife, Maureen wouldn't object. Guess what his kids, all younger than six years of age, acknowledged as the father's role in a family. Fortunately, the five-year-old knew enough to start questioning his father's behavior, based on how he saw other dads treat their children with loving kindness. This helped free him later from the bonds of implicit and explicit memory in rearing his own children.

Freud coined a psychological term, "repetition compulsion," to describe our drive to duplicate our earlier relationship patterns. In a sense, we are our parents' children, now parents ourselves. It is an emotional legacy we pass on to our descendents unless interrupted. The way we were treated as infants has an uncanny way of being passed on to our own offspring. How we respond to our young child's behavior is likely similar to how our parents responded to our behavior. The main difference is the inevitable change that occurs in a developing society or culture. But we, now as parents, probably continue to embrace what we experienced as children, without ever thinking about it.

As with Margaret and Sean, what legacy do we leave for our children and later descendants, based on how we were treated as children? Please pardon the philosophical suggestion, but souls and humans are biologically and spiritually capable of unceasing care and love for our Creator, our family, and other people. However, the behavior we manifest is subject to the ebb and flow of human nature.

Is it possible that much of the persisting ethnic prejudice is "hereditary?" We are told that concerns about personal security often foster intolerance. It might be a natural instinct passed on from generation to generation. But with competition rampant for power, affluence, and status, snobbery is a natural by-product. A major social problem does exist, however. Ethnic stereotypes may persist in depriving persons of different backgrounds an equal opportunity to contribute to society and to be rewarded accordingly. Unfortunately, there still seems to be an element of society that disavows acknowledging the examples of persons who have succeeded and been recognized despite their ethnic background. Interestingly, those protestors often have the same ethnic heritage as the role models whose achievements they conveniently disallow. This protest element seems to seek to perpetuate an image of rampant societal prejudice, discrimination, and injustice. Is their professed discontent intended only to serve their own personal recognition and reward?

In the sixties and seventies, persons promoting "enlightenment" introduced Americans of all ethnic backgrounds to mind-distorting drugs. How reminiscent this was; many Native American tribes were peace loving until our American forefathers introduced them to alcohol. There were economic benefits for a few and horrible consequences for many others. Today we see similar victims caught in the snares of profiteering drug lords. In a sense, how much does substance abuse (e.g., alcohol, cocaine, and medications) perpetuate improper implicit images in our young people of social—not moral—acceptability of such substances?

Working Mothers: By Their Choice?

Obviously, part of the stimulus for young mothers to work outside the home today is a need for additional family income. For many years, however, some mothers considered their parental responsibilities mundane and under-appreciated. Many longed for opportunities to delegate these roles to caregivers and to let their other talents blossom outside the home.

The April 28, 2008, issue of *Newsweek* carried an article by Jennie Yabroff, "The Feminine Mistakes," which reviewed the book *Opting In: Having a Child Without Losing Yourself* by Amy Richards. The article notes an interesting aspect of almost any group discussion by young mothers about the idea of working versus staying at home with children. The focus eventually turned to their mothers. This didn't involve differing attitudes between the daughters and their mothers. Rather, it apparently centered on the participants' feelings about how they recall being reared: by working or stay-at-home mothers.

How much of the feelings of today's young mothers about working moms came from their own mothers' behavior? Their mothers' choices of working instead of nurturing may have shaped their daughters' attitudes from their early childhood. For example, it seems conceivable that some of their mothers exhibited an obvious distaste for the obligations and restrictions of motherhood. Others may have flourished in it without complaints. From all you have read so far, isn't it reasonable that their mothers' behavior shaped their daughters' beliefs about motherhood, without their daughters even realizing it?

With the advent of women's rights and feminist movements, imagine the potential tensions these may have created with implicit, unrealized, programmed attitudes present in these young women. Such inner conflicts apparently could provoke all sorts of deviant mental states as inner wars erupted around "doing the right thing."

Mothers committed to remaining at home, as well as mothers who led successful careers, may have created role models that their daughters find difficult to match. Young women reared in poverty, especially if implicitly convinced of their lack of worth or motivation, may simply serve as "baby mills" and, as a result, depend on welfare entitlements.

You never expected our lives to be so complicated? You think maybe this book will tell you more than you want to know? The next chapter will let you "off the hook," so to speak.

CHAPTER THREE

SO WHAT?

Can't You Just Be Yourself?

YES. HONESTLY, YOU CAN. SOME people seem to be in perfect harmony with themselves, with others, and with life itself. They should not be reading this book. It may risk rupturing that harmony by creating internal doubts. After all, if you're at peace with yourself, with others, and with your environment, why disturb it?

Buddhist monks may appear to be deprived of what more materialistic people consider the "good life." But these spiritually devoted individuals exemplify perhaps the epitome of being at peace, with themselves, with others, and with their environments. True, one might question how these people can be "at peace" in the face of oppression by neighboring governments. Still, there are many monks who take this in stride.

Reality is a tough subject to discuss. Each of us is convinced we have a proper—perhaps the only real—view of it. But perception is a tough taskmaster. No doubt you've seen artwork that you're convinced depicts a specific image. Try a different perspective, and you may find that it appears to be entirely different.

Consider some homeless people. They may even refuse an offer of permanent shelter. Do-gooders may actually offend them. Is it because they are ashamed of their homeless states? Or are they resentful of would-be helpers' self-righteous approach? They too are susceptible to the inner and external influences that shape all our lives. It's notable that some homeless persons formerly pursued successful careers and apparently led satisfying lives. Perhaps the long reach of early childhood experiences eventually uprooted their security.

It's been shown that near-death experiences often changed the lives of survivors so dramatically that family members and friends refused to accept their new personality. Some thought them to have become mentally deranged for being less devoted to materialism, more benevolent, and spiritually inclined. Family and friends' persistent failure to accept these personality changes eventually drove some survivors to alcoholism or suicide.

Despite the failure by some family members or acquaintances to accept such dramatic change in near-death survivors, widespread interest in life change persists. Thousands of self-help books have appeared in bookstores. Religious leaders and therapists have insisted on life renovations. But there seems to remain a question about how effective such efforts are to reach unrecognized parts of a person's "self." Apparently self-help may fall short of near-death experiences in truly changing lives.

Apparently, some people reach a point in their lives at which they experience what might be called a "serendipitous awakening." This is said to occur when they

- start to wonder about their purpose for living,
- challenge competitive materialism, or
- catch a glimpse of the sublime.

It is a state of mind that might be called transcendence, a concept involving progress toward personal potential. This may have been spiritually endowed or a surprise revelation from their implicit memories. Nevertheless, it seems to have the potential positively to change that person's life. I hope that Pastor Joel Osteen would agree that any actualization of personal potential remains between the individual and God, and it depends on that individual sharing both the decision and the responsibility. Has it ever occurred to you that we may have been endowed, as are all living things, with an almost infinite potential, as part of the act of creation? Furthermore, whatever we pray for actually doesn't depend on our believing that it will be granted, but on our believing instead that, if we personally commit ourselves, unseen help will guide us toward achieving our goals.

This emphasizes the significance of what we think of ourselves: our self-esteem and our self-potential. It involves our relationships with others and within ourselves. It looks at our spiritual side as well as our material side. It is grounded in the advancing scientific research. Moreover, it looks not only at us, but also at others, especially those whose lives we can positively influence. It thereby also provides a perspective for both natural and adoptive parents, into whose care newborn humans are entrusted.

Free Will: Really?

Have you ever consciously tried to do or say something but found that it came out wrong? If so, you may have been surprised and just disregarded it, not knowing why.

For example, studies on racial or ethnic prejudice have shown that many people who disavow being prejudiced actually act in the opposite manner. If they truly had free will to make and act on conscious choices, this conflicting behavior would not happen. We are told that offspring typically adopt their parents' or family's attitude, or the predominant attitude of their group or culture. But if this is part of their subconscious implicit programmed responses, it may remain with them for life.

The idea of "free will" has been debated throughout history. Many views have been expressed about free will. Could it be possible that free will is accessible only as long as humankind is aware of, and is able to escape from, the restraints of programmed implicit behavior?

Scientists studying the origin of intent in the brain discovered a fascinating fact. This involved having subjects lift their fingers when they felt an urge to do so. The finger and the brain of each subject were wired to recording devices as was the perceived urge. A delay of one second was found before subjects lifted their fingers after a readiness potential was recorded in the brain. But the readiness potential was shown to exist two hundred milliseconds before the urge existed. This suggested that before the brain sent an impulse to the finger, something in the brain happened to provide a readiness potential. In other words, there apparently was an unconscious anticipation of the action.

Therefore, is the choice made in the brain before we decide to act? Is there such a thing as free will? Was there an unconscious involvement? Only in the intervening two hundred milliseconds was consciousness involved; hence, there was free decision or free will at that point. It seems that the brain had veto power over the event, leading researchers to say, "There is no such thing as free will, but there is a free won't." In his book *The Illusion of Conscious Will*, Daniel Wegner posed a question about the experimental results described above. He asks whether the brain anticipates an action and prepares for it, without our conscious awareness. This seems to raise the perennial question, is the mind independent of the brain?

As mentioned earlier, implicit behavioral responses occur unintentionally and without conscious awareness. Researchers and even Freud seemed to believe that the source of these is the unconscious (subconscious) mind. If true, perhaps the anticipation of an event occurs in the subconscious mind and signals the brain to be ready. Regardless of the process, Wegner stresses, we are reminded that we all are responsible for our decisions and behavior.

Making Choices

Tangential to the idea of free will is the process of making decisions or choices based upon our individual preferences. Memory is naturally implicated here. A theory known as preferences-as-memory (PAM) says that our preferences are neither completely stable over time nor made anew for each choice we make. Instead, it describes preference as a "lumpy and discontinuous" process that reacts to external stimuli and is the result of a person's reasoning from among choices available. PAM implies the involvement of *explicit* memory and excludes, by definition, *implicit* memory. In their paper "Constructing Preferences from Memory," Elke Weber and Eric Johnson acknowledge that a number of researchers have begun to differentiate between the two memory systems.

All the while, there is that backdrop to everything we do called implicit memory or implicit self-esteem. But this fact is not an indictment that each of us is a helpless victim of our environment! Instead, I believe it encourages us to find a middle ground: we can control our lives by acknowledging that we are seldom aware of all the facts and options about any circumstance. We may never fully identify the nature or cause of our programmed emotional responses. However, that doesn't prevent us from recognizing their potential impact in cases like those discussed later as "disruptions of a natural process." No wonder many mental health professionals now seem to believe that the treatment of many mental illnesses must include considering the impact of implicit memory.

So you decided to stay with us? The next chapter will take you inside the human minds. (Yes, plural!)

Chapter Four

Our Multiple Minds

It appears that memory is not a thing, but a process. Conscious memory is initiated by an external stimulus or an internal intention, and each memory is a composite of the event, the stimulus or intention, and often an emotion. For some reason, emotions can be stored with an associated memory.

It is now generally recognized that when a child is born, he or she is fully capable of *experiencing* almost all of the emotions of adults. Researchers tell us that newborns can express rage, jealousy, anger, love, and sadness. But newborns' emotions are sensed differently from those of teenagers and adults. We are consciously aware of the distinctive nature of feeling emotions, such as anger, joy, fear, jealousy, and revenge. Sometimes we know the reasons behind them. By contrast, the infant's ability to reason, recognize, and evaluate doesn't develop for some time. But sensations or feelings seem to exist even before birth.

Imagine a teenager who becomes pregnant either from unprotected repeated sex or in a sudden moment of ecstasy. She confronts the father, who disavows responsibility and jettisons her from his life. Nothing in her young life has prepared her for this moment. The stress plays havoc with her body's biochemicals and is relayed to the fetus through the placenta. Even though the fetal body is immature, it senses a sort of alarm, probably associated with primal emotions. The fetus's somatic (cellular) memory is activated. Subsequent physical or mental events for the mother can not only register in the fetus's physiology but also be retained in fetal implicit memory.

There is increasing evidence that early experiences in life may affect neural pathways and components to shape responses to daily events. As unbelievable as it may sound, there are theories that the human mind, with its implicit memory, exists before the nervous system develops.

Let's go back to the distinction between implicit and explicit memory. We often consider memory as something that can be recalled at will. This is true with explicit memory. With implicit memory, neither the event nor the time can be intentionally or consciously remembered. But it may be imprinted in our subconscious mind with an associated emotion, similar to a tape or disc recording. This makes it uncontrollably influential or automatic in determining our responses to environmental stimuli. Even little things such as the way somebody grins or smirks at us may evoke an unconscious reaction.

Neurobiology

Canadian researchers have provided a very detailed scientific explanation of neural pathways the brain uses to distinguish between implicit and explicit reactions to stimuli. It is entitled "The Brain from Top to Bottom: The Amygdala and Its Allies" and is provided by The Canadian Institutes of Health Research and the Canadian Institute of Neurosciences, Mental Health, and Addiction.

The amygdalae (there are a pair) actually seem to moderate all our responses, both emotional and behavioral, to stimuli involving our survival, including security, threat, and even rivals. Our amygdalae are vital to feeling certain emotions and to sensing them in other people. Scientists have found that stimuli from our senses may go directly to the amygdalae rather than through sensory evaluation mechanisms. The latter would traditionally allow us to recognize and evaluate what's happening and to respond accordingly. The amygdalae are mature at birth and unconsciously can exert significant influences on children and adults. Neural systems that allow rational control of emotions don't seem to mature until early adulthood. Traumas that occurred in early childhood still can disturb mental and behavioral functions in an adult through implicit memories he or she doesn't recognize.

Between twelve and twenty-four months of age, another part of the brain, known as the hippocampus, starts to mature. It is responsible for explicit memory. We are told that facts and experiences typically become part of our conscious (explicit) memory around age three or four. Some researchers say this occurs earlier. At the time explicit memories occur, we are aware of them, and we usually can recall them later. By contrast, it appears that we were not even aware when an implicit event and its accompanying emotion were stored in our subconscious memory.

Intention

Psychology defines the conscious (explicit) mind in three subdivisions: cognition, affect, and conation. It seems worthwhile to examine these as stages of sorts that happen before action of any kind is taken. We know cognition better by the terms *knowing* and *understanding*. It's an awareness of receiving, storing, processing, and retrieving information. Affect is more familiar as emotions. Conation is the thought process that builds intention upon cognition and affect. Conation is vital for a person to be successful in self-direction and self-regulation. In short, we learn and consider something. Almost simultaneously, we feel a certain way about it. Then we decide what action, if any, to take as a result. Intention is sometimes related to the question of free will—conceivably the amount of control we have on conation.

Physical or Mental Child Abuse

Even though most of us sensed the love of our mothers as young babies, there probably were times when our mothers were stressed and passed the emotion on to us. Some mothers even have physically abused their children or taunted them with verbal abuse. The youngster naturally reacts emotionally. If this mistreatment becomes customary, the child may develop a defensive emotional response. This could be incorporated into his or her self-image. Abuse may register in implicit and explicit states of mind, depending on the child's age.

Since mistreatment can be mental as well as physical, a very young child who is repeatedly berated by parents may develop a low implicit self-esteem. Mistakenly, he or she firmly may believe that the accusations are true. Shame and guilt may accompany these beliefs. If a parent belittles a very young child as worthless, imagine the lack of motivation hidden in the youngster's implicit memory. By contrast, unrealistic expectations may be programmed into the implicit memory of a child who is continually praised.

But actual abuse does not have to be repeated later in life to stimulate or "prime" the emotion. Maltreatment involves a variety of specifics, such as who, where, when, and how. So the victim might unconsciously manifest the same emotion later in life when he or she again encounters anything reminiscent of the specifics. That may control the person's behavioral response without his or her actual awareness of the imprinted event or emotion. The Veterans Administration diagnoses posttraumatic stress syndrome (PTSS) as being enhanced by abuse early in patients' lives.

An example of stress on the mother passed on to the fetus or child might be an unwanted child. It is said that young children are very sensitive to parental behavior and that certain behaviors carry implications for the child. It seems unlikely that a child would ever ask, "Why didn't you want me?" But a child easily may sense parents' negativity and incorporate a related emotion into his or her self-image. This might include a false impression that he or she somehow was to blame.

The bottom line is that each of us has formed and stored certain memories and response mechanisms. These are like tape or disc recordings, retained in something postulated to be a "subconscious mind." These automatic response mechanisms can be activated, or primed, later in life. Environmental stimuli include people, places, and things and can occur without conscious recall of the earlier events or awareness of their effects on us.

Conscious (Explicit) Memory

With explicit memory, you consciously may be aware of anger you feel toward a person or about a happening. You also may know what causes that feeling. Apparently, this ability to recognize and reason through an explicit emotion is fully developed by young adulthood. How well the person deals with the emotion remains to be seen. We may be aware of past events and explicit memories that remind us of them. For example, a memory of someone who used to bully me may cause my sense of distrust for a person who reminds me of him. If that individual is my demanding boss, I consciously may feel that he is "bullying" me.

Consciousness

Scientists still seem to find consciousness an enigma: it apparently is highly individualized for each of us. We differ in how we personally experience our awareness of the world around us. Scientists therefore have been unable precisely to define the neurological map of consciousness.

Consciousness, you may say, is nothing more than observing, thinking, and choosing. It naturally may seem to be centered in the brain and involve complex brain functions. The brain obviously must be involved in some aspects of consciousness, such as explicit memory. But a form of consciousness has been documented in situations in which heart and brain waves cease to exist. In his book *In Search of Memory: The Emergence of a New Science of Mind*, Eric Kandel said, "Consciousness in people is an awareness of self, an awareness of being aware."

According to Joseph Sandler, Sigmund Freud identified three "principles and foundations" that must be recognized as the cornerstones of psychoanalytic theory. Notably, the first was the assumption of unconscious mental processes. The second was the recognition of the theory of resistance and repression. The third was the acknowledgment of the importance of sexuality and the Oedipus complex. It had been demonstrated that certain common mental acts by normal people had meanings that were unknown to the person. But this meaning could be revealed through analytic means. Hypnosis was one way experimentally to prove the existence of such unconscious mental acts.

Conscious Mind

Obviously, the conscious mind is the mental state in which we spend the majority of our waking hours. Although science has been unable to conclude that our awareness occurs in the brain, each of us knows it exists. Perhaps the most confusing aspect of the conscious mind is how individualized the perceptions of reality that it creates are. Virtually no two people have an identical mental picture simultaneously. This is a key to what makes each of us unique.

While some people have claimed to be able to "read" minds, there is no credible evidence that they actually can "see" what we perceive in our awareness. One reason for this could be the fleeting nature of our attention spans in our hectic daily lives. Also, research has shown that we unconsciously and unintentionally may shift to using our subconscious or superconscious minds.

Rupert Sheldrake's book *The Hypothesis of a New Science of Life: Morphic Resonance* includes an unusual claim. "In the mechanistic theory of life, the conscious self has been seen as a sort of 'ghost in the machine.'" In the absence of a materialistic explanation of consciousness, certain assumptions are made. Among them is that consciousness interacts with the brain, the body, and the environment through energy fields, in perceiving and directing human activity. The reason is that forms of consciousness have been demonstrated in comatose or brain-dead patients as well as in dreams, where environmental influence and human activity basically are absent. A discussion of such fields appears later in this book.

Self-Consciousness

Humankind seems to be the only animal in which self-consciousness has been manifested. However, certain species of animals do demonstrate something akin to consciousness. In the fascinating book *When Elephants Weep,* by Jeffrey Moussaieff Masson and Susan McCarthy, the authors provide a compelling account of examples. These suggest that animals may have awareness and emotions that resemble a form of consciousness. Although presented from the antivivisectionist's point of view, Masson and McCarthy's *New York Times* best seller was a powerful protagonist for recognizing that emotions and consciousness may not be limited to humans.

As ubiquitous as self-consciousness is, it may manifest itself in many ways. I may

- dwell on how I feel about my physical appearance and attractiveness to others,
- shortchange myself by believing that I can't achieve some particular goal, or
- discount compliments by convincing myself that I don't deserve them.

In contrast, I may

- try to inflate my ego by certain words or actions,
- rationalize my behavior as justifiable, or
- disregard potential consequences as unlikely or a worthwhile risk.

Free will seems accessible only through having the presence of mind to *self-consciously* step back and assess our feelings about anyone or anything. It's been said that we count our miseries carefully, but disregard our blessings; also, that we mentally re-live our failures and forget our successes.

You may have heard the words "attention" and "intention." Attention simply means focusing only on what's happening at the moment. Naturally, our hectic lifestyles almost forbid it. Often, you may feel a so-called "gut reaction" and respond a certain way. Intention, however, means to choose on your own what decision to make or action to take. Notice that there is a bridge between focusing on the moment and intention: self-consciousness. This seems to be the ability to confront impulsive responses in light of current circumstances, to evaluate options, and to decide what to do.

Subconscious (Unconscious) Mind

In his online article, Michael Mathews addressed "Freud's Consciousness and the Unconscious." Some scientists now divide the latter into subconscious and superconscious states of mind. Implicit memory is said to exist in the subconscious mind, inaccessible to conscious recall but controlling our behavior automatically.

Superconscious Mind

Some researchers consider the superconscious mind to be the residence of the soul, with access to a "universal consciousness." This is the level that certain researchers have been able to reach through special approaches in hypnotic past-life regression. If and when conscience, imagination, intuition, and inspiration are manifested by the mind, it is said that they originate in the superconscious mind. In her book *Infinite Mind: Science of the Human Vibrations of Consciousness*, Valerie Hunt quoted three eminent neurophysiologists, Penfield, Eccles, and Granit. They felt that the abilities inherent in the higher levels of the mind include insight, intuition, imagination, creativity, reasoning, will, intent, decision, and soul.

The Conscious Universe

As you see, our so-called multiple minds are simply three levels of mind. Moreover, the three are not separate entities. "Doors" exist between them, much as doors exist between separate rooms in a house. This makes each level accessible according to the state of awareness we have at a given time. Hypnosis seems to facilitate passage through these doors, as do certain mental exercises such as meditation. Even if our mind is considered a three-level entity, consciousness remains an enigma.

Some leading-edge researchers have suggested the existence of a universal consciousness. In other words, it could be a sort of matrix that connects all existence. Conceptually, this might be a nonphysical dimension that we might perceive only in higher levels of the mind.

But consciousness seems unlikely ever to be defined scientifically. If that is true, consider the possibility that the God we endow with human qualities was, is, and "exists" as the essence and source of all consciousness. As much a stretch of our imagination as this may be, it certainly seems beyond scientific proof.

Ever wonder how much of "you" depends on your surroundings and your circumstances? The next chapter helps explain this and may surprise you!

Chapter Five

Our Environment

The term "environment" is used often in this book. It is not intended in the same context as environmental concern about global warming or threats to wildlife. Rather, the environment of a cell, organ, human being, pregnancy, fetus, child, teenager, or adult is the nature of its, his, or her surroundings. This includes people, circumstances, and things. There is such a variety of specifics that it is impossible to list all of them.

Perhaps this is best considered by thinking of absolutely everything that might characterize the setting of a pregnancy, from "a" (abalone) to "z" (zydeco). I use this expression to emphasize the inclusion of small, sometimes seemingly insignificant, considerations.

Hundreds of years ago, our environment was limited to our surroundings and occasional news from other places. Today, our same environment has become exceedingly complex. Only when we sleep do we escape being bombarded by thousands of demands for our attention. Don't try to count—statistically they exist!

So what's the impact? Sensory overload, inadequate opportunity to evaluate, and memory dysfunction. It seems literally impossible to process adequately the barrage of inputs from people, circumstances, news media, and commercials. Family, friends, business clients and associates, neighbors, teachers, and ministers multiply people demands—the list is endless.

Imagine too how the sensory burden is multiplied by the business concept of "multitasking." Apparently, efficiency experts decided that having workers perform multiple tasks concurrently could increase output or efficiency. Thus, a fast-food counter clerk is waiting for a hamburger to be cooked and wrapped. But after the customer has paid, that clerk could be taking another order or performing other tasks, not just standing idle.

Ancient Guardians

Eons ago, evolution introduced some surprising survival mechanisms. Discovered in fruit flies in 1962, these were thought to be unique to the species. Not until fifteen years later were they detected in other forms of life. They go by the name "heat shock proteins" (HSPs), which is a sort of misnomer. This comes from their initially being observed in fruit flies where the temperature of their environment had been artificially raised.

Dr. Pramod K. Srivastava told the story of the remarkable HSPs in his article "New Jobs for Ancient Chaperones" in the July 2008 issue of *Scientific American.* The most amazing aspect of these proteins is not their value in preserving human life but their wide range of protective effects. These have been found to be central to life itself, for their role in protecting vital genetic and protein synthesis functions. Their potential preventive and therapeutic use in medicine seems unparalleled.

HSPs have been ubiquitous over millions of years in cells and organisms. The key to understanding HSPs is the concept of protein synthesis. This is basic to human development and growth patterned after the DNA blueprint. Protein synthesis is beyond the scope of this book. An excellent primer on protein synthesis is Bruce Lipton's *The Biology of Belief: Understanding the Power of Conscious, Matter, and Miracles* (2005).

People

This well could be the most influential facet of our environment, from conception to death. Exceptions occur, where things or circumstances prevail. But our interpersonal relationships with other people add the unique dimension of your and their uncertain agendas.

This dimension is not involved when we're working with things and even when we're interacting with animals. Things and animals have no personal agenda. Tara Parker-Pope illustrated this with her article "Better Health, Down on the Farm" in the July 1, 2008, edition of the

New York Times. Researchers found that working with farm animals may improve mental health of patients with psychiatric illnesses.

The same finding was reported for problem kids at day camps and difficult residents of penal institutions. In some instances, simply putting a kid or an inmate in charge of a dog gave him or her a reason for living. It rewarded the person with unrestricted love in return. With children who were having coping problems, pairing each child with a dog that also had psychological problems worked wonders for both of them. Apparently, the child recognized that the animal had problems similar to his or hers and the two soon bonded.

This may validate the hypothesis that dealing with other people presents a challenge not faced in relationships with animals. Animals do not question our motives; they accept us as we are; they don't compete with us; and they reward us with unconditional affection. Obviously, this is not the case with pets abused or abandoned by their owners.

With regard to better mental health on the farm, contrast that setting with a busy metropolitan area. The latter creates a continuing stress on the individual, but the farm is idyllic by comparison.

Family

It seems inconceivable that anything or anyone else has as much influence on a fetus or child as its mother. This has seemed to be nature's intent forever, manifested in both humans and animals. It seems like a reciprocal relationship: we learn from our offspring and they learn from us.

It may be questioned how much adults learn from children. Perhaps it is not a matter of what or how much we learn, but our attitude toward it. We are expected to respect what child development and health professionals tell us. It's almost as if there were a standard of behavior that mothers are supposed to accept from conception forward. There naturally is the chance that this will become so regimented that mothers perform it too mechanically.

That conclusion is not to disallow that nature ensures a strong personal bond between mother and infant. But nature needs maternal support. This bond may be the strongest affinity ever experienced by humankind. But disruptions can occur in the process of birthing and nurturing. Moreover, societal demands or personal choices often are allowed to interfere with the fulfillment of this bond.

As you read earlier, it used to be accepted as fact that no memory is retained from the prenatal and neonatal periods of life, a so-called infantile amnesia. Now it is acknowledged that fetuses and infants have one memory system that forms even in the womb and another system that doesn't develop for a couple of years. Whether fortunate or not for the infant, the first system subconsciously seems to register experiences and associated emotions. Yet the impact of the first system may be even more profound than the second: the first one cannot intentionally be recalled, and yet it shapes automatic responses by the individual later in life.

Thus it is for the fetus and the newborn. A sensation similar to hearing has been demonstrated in fetuses from early in gestation. Levels of various biochemicals in the mother's body change in response to her mood, and these influence the fetus too during fluid exchange through the placenta. So, even before birth, the fetus is sensitive to factors in the environment that affect the mother's mental state as well as her physical health.

Peers

Second only to family is the significant influence that peers exert. It seems safe to assume that peers establish norms required for group acceptance and peer recognition. Rejection can be an almost insurmountable obstacle for personal explicit self-esteem. It seems indeterminate how fully this quest is dependent upon an individual's *implicit* self-esteem. This could depend on the individual's unconscious perception of his or her standing in the family versus his or her blossoming desire for independence. In other words, did the family or nature foster peer attraction?

Significant Others

This term usually means a partner, a trusted friend, or another person whose standing is such that his or her views are considered unquestionable. This need not depend upon the significant other's relationship, educational or economic status, or other qualifications. It is more the product of an individual's favorable perception of and trust in the significant other.

One remarkable case involved a couple who wisely realized that their children might have questions or concerns they felt uncomfortable discussing with Mom and Dad. The parents got permission from another, very close and trusted couple with whom they knew the kids felt intimate. Then the parents explained to their children that this other couple should be considered confidants. The siblings could discuss anything with that couple, and it would not be disclosed to the parents.

All Others

Every child and adult is consciously and unconsciously influenced by a wide assortment of other people throughout their lives. Some of this is intentional instruction, as in schools and churches. Some of it is less formal, such as those persons expressing a view or passing on something they were told. You'll read later about something researchers are calling "source memory," where an unfounded assertion of fact can be spread widely as a rumor or gossip.

Star Power

This involves a person's feeling, even his or her conviction, which elevates him or her above all others. As you'll read later, this may manifest itself in egocentricity or even narcissism. This may result as a natural product of how he or she was reared. But it also can come from a person's self-aggrandizement, stimulated by adoring followers. This is a sinister force in today's world, which literally can convince an otherwise normal person that he or she is invincible. This can be very subtle, even unrecognized by the individual. It may be gradual or overwhelmingly fast. It may be unstoppable.

Senator John Edwards expressed this reasoning in a television interview to justify his unfaithfulness to his wife, Elizabeth, during his 2008 campaign for the Democratic presidential nomination. He felt beyond accountability to anyone. One must wonder how much of this "star power" overcomes stage, screen, and music stars, and even sports figures and politicians. We need only to watch the news to see how many public figures let this spoil their opportunity to be upstanding role models and world benefactors.

Society

Perhaps the most immutable influence on a person is his or her society or culture. Remember that nature's purpose for implicit memory is to prepare a newborn for coping in the natural parents' setting. But the so-called society is composed not only of people but also of ever-changing standards and practices. The latter seem to ebb and flow without uniform consensus. The section on generational influences illustrates this.

Religion and Health Care

This may be the most controversial part of this book. It was distilled from Pearce's book *The Biology of Transcendence: A Blueprint of the Human Spirit* (2002) and from reports by other authors. In a sense, Pearce's book tracks attitudes toward conception, childbirth, nurturing, and caregivers in relevant historical times and our resulting departure from natural mothering.

Early theologians designated the fall of Adam in the Garden of Eden as man's original sin and somehow linked it with subsequent conception of humankind. Childbirth was held to require pain and suffering. The reigning clergy demonized midwives who helped make childbirth easy and shared their female wisdom with new mothers. Lengthy hospital stays formerly required for mothers initiated long separations between mother and newborn, often interrupting mother-child bonding with long stays in the hospital nursery. This sometimes interspersed or replaced breast-feeding with bottle-feeding and made bottle-feeding both socially and medically acceptable.

Interestingly, in the October 2008 *Medscape,* Barclay and Vega prepared a continuing medical education program, "Counseling Interventions Recommended to Promote and Support Breast-Feeding." It focused on "The U. S. Preventive Services Task Force (USPSTF) ... updated statement recommending counseling interventions during pregnancy and after birth to promote and support breast-feeding. The updated guidelines and evidence review are published in the October 21, 2008, issue of the *Annals of Internal Medicine.*" The USPSTF statement is based on a study that shows that breast-feeding offers significant health benefits for both the mother and the baby. The American Academy of Pediatrics said, "some of the obstacles to initiation and continuation of breastfeeding include insufficient prenatal education about breastfeeding, disruptive maternity care practices, and lack of family and broad societal support."

Workplace Stress

Working in a stressful environment obviously can create problems for teenagers and adults. There are tensions between employees; between employees and superiors; between friends; and, perhaps most important, between parents. These can be sparked by and taken home from the workplace, then noted with concern by the children. A young son or daughter easily may misinterpret spousal arguments to be his or her fault, especially if the eventual result is divorce. Children also may misunderstand loss of a job by either spouse, a forced move to another town, inability to meet financial obligations, and many other crises.

Setting

This is nothing more than the geographical place in which an infant is born, complete with all the specific details that characterize it. Contrast a middle-class farm in rural Nebraska with a crowded small flat in New York City or with a wealthy suburban estate in Bucks County, Pennsylvania.

Eat, Drink, and Be What?

Common sense says that whatever we eat, drink, or otherwise take in is dangerous only because of what it is. In other words, vitamins exert their effect only as such, and radiator fluid is poisonous. But there is a new science, "metabolomics," which promises to reveal all manner of unexpected effects from what we ingest due to variation in human metabolism. This was revealed in an article "Going With His Gut Bacteria" in the July 2008 issue of *Scientific American*. The author, researcher Jeremy Nicholson, is reputed to be one of the world's foremost experts in this new field.

Nicholson uses a process known as nuclear magnetic resonance spectroscopy to identify specific chemicals that are produced in our bodies as metabolites. These are the many different substances that might result from chemically breaking down whatever we take in. There are ten trillion bacteria of a thousand species in our intestinal tract, which are responsible for this. Apparently the substances produced can vary according to an individual's genetic makeup, thus individualizing the potential impact of these metabolites on our bodies. Metabolomics, and its cousin, "metabonomics"—the results of individualization and stress on metabolic systems—offer new promise for preventive and therapeutic medicines.

Electronic Devices

The advent of single-person or remote participant electronic devices probably has had a significant environmental impact on child rearing, growth, and development. It might be impossible to overestimate their long-term influence on humankind. Examples are plentiful and their interference is often publicized. Online predators, game addicts, and classroom cheating are among a multitude of potentially nefarious outcomes. Yet, much disagreement exists throughout the world about the impact of these devices.

But there also is a more insidious potential outcome of our increasing dependence on electronic information sourcing and processing. Michael Merzenich described this in his post "Going Googly." This is based upon research documentation that "brains grow and elaborate and strengthen when they are challenged and that they change little when solutions are easy to come by." Computer and electronic device devotees may challenge this threat. But most of them likely will agree that these devices should not replace but stimulate use of the human brain. One example that seems questionable might be the use of first calculators, then computers, to teach mathematics, since this subject in the raw encourages analysis and reasoning. Unfortunately, it seems impossible to predict the extent of potentially dire consequences of allowing machines to do our thinking.

Information Overload

Many people agree that electronics have made many positive contributions to the modern world. Yet some researchers fear that the demands these innovations impose on human beings eventually might wreak havoc on mankind. Yet, the welcome accorded these technological advances often blinds us to warnings from those who might be called "Chicken Little" researchers.

For example, four thousand test subjects in their late teens to early twenties were involved in a twenty-year longitudinal study. Pearce (2002) cited researchers' discovery that the subjects' sensitivity to stimuli decreased about 1 percent per year. This began in the 1960s in Germany, so imagine where we must be today. There also appeared something called a "new indifference," in which the brain couldn't resolve contradictory pieces of information and therefore treated everything with a low-grade response.

The language translation of the Germans' conclusion was that, for our brains to register it, "brutal thrill" stimuli are required. Marnia Robinson discussed this in "The Brutish Brain." Technically, it appeared that these subjects had been exposed to high-intensity stimuli from birth, often without appropriate early nurturing and natural development of their reticular activating system (RAS).

The RAS is described as the place where and process by which sensory input into the body is organized before being sent to higher brain centers for processing. There apparently is an RAS threshold or minimum level that stimuli must exceed to be of sufficient intensity to register in conscious awareness and perception. Said another way, it seems that people are becoming much less aware of subtle happenings around them. (http://www.rnceus.com/uncon/ununcon.html.) It has been claimed that young people today typically require a high-level stimulus or else succumb to anxiety or depression. Many avoid a leisurely hike in the mountains or a day at the zoo. They feel deprived of the accustomed, fast-paced, intense stimuli needed to keep their awareness functioning.

The July 29, 2008, *Oprah Show* alerted parents to deadly consequences that can result from what's called the "choking game." It's also referred to as the "fainting game." A startling 2008 report came from the Ontario Centre for Addiction and Mental Health. It found that at least seventy-nine thousand students in the Canadian province of Ontario had participated in this act. This involves cutting off the supply of oxygen to the brain. Some kids experiment with strangling themselves with rope. They may be alone, with no one else present to keep this from turning fatal. Obviously, the participant must be resuscitated quickly. This may result from peer pressure or anticipation of a unique physiological sensation. But it must be questioned whether this exemplifies the "brutal thrill" young people are said to require for sufficient stimulation.

One caution many researchers have issued addresses the growing use of computers by young people whose early nurturing and development was incomplete. Technology may be advancing so fast that inadequately maturing brains are at high risk for keeping pace. Yet secondary—and even primary—education seems intent on cramming more information into the curricula by requiring students to be computer savvy.

As far back as 1991, Marcia Mikulak published some remarkable findings in her book *The Children of a Bombara Village*. It compared children of primitive societies with those of industrial-technological countries. The former were twenty-five to 30 percent more sensitive to sensory inputs and more consciously aware of their surroundings than the latter!

In Pearce's book *Evolution's End* (1991), he quoted from studies in the late 1980s that compared "deprived" children in economically depressed so-called primitive societies with our "well-cared-for" children. When the former were put into learning environments like ours, they exhibited three to four times higher learning capacity than our children, including rate of attention, comprehension, and retention. The conclusion was that these deprived children had been given the only thing that their culture could afford: loving care, attention, and nurturing.

Dropout rates in our schools are a constant topic among educators today. Proposed remedies are varied. But two considerations seem overlooked: information overload and student indifference. In the studies Pearce quoted, what might have been the role of the young persons' perceptions of the value and accessibility of education? Nurturing, or lack of it, obviously contributed to the difference between the two groups. Nevertheless, the deprived children might have been eager to learn if given the opportunity. This love for learning seems lacking in many of today's students.

This still doesn't solve information overload, which begins at home in pre-school years. Today's homes are loaded with electronic devices that confront kids before they can walk or talk.

Cyber-Disinhibition

Cyberspace poses a unique problem for teens and young adults. It involves "cyber-disinhibition." This correlates two scientific facts. First, much communication via the Internet and cell talk-picture phones is unilateral. That is, a message/picture may be sent to another person, apparently even anonymously. This message/picture may be such that the sender would never say or show it to the person receiving it face-to-face. Face-to-face, there is an audible and visible feedback that characteristically confines the sender to certain guidelines. Face-to-face, if the sender said or showed something that elicited tears, criticism, or even fisticuffs from the receiver, that reciprocal action—or even an anticipation of it—might modify the sender's behavior. Second, the key inhibitory mechanism that guides our conduct toward others is located in the prefrontal cortex. It is one of the last parts of the brain to become fully mature, usually during our twenties. Adolescence is a period not only of ripe impulsivity but also of immature inhibition.

Cyber-bullying and sexual exhibition are just two of the manifestations of cyber-disinhibition. It may be possible for modern technology to track the source of cell talk-picture phone transmissions. But it still seems difficult, if not impossible, to trace Internet child predators and teenage hackers. Cyber-disinhibition apparently provides violators with a perceived illusiveness that fosters a stimulating challenge of wits.

Commercialism

In a free-enterprise country like ours, consumers drive our economy. Manufacturers and retailers therefore use almost every conceivable kind of advertising. Since most ads appear true to life, some may produce unintended consequences. Even the nature of an advertisement can elicit an unconscious and unintentional internal or behavioral response. Television ads typically portray ostensibly desirable real-life standards. Naturally, these ads involve personal and family standing, economic status, dress code, body image, livelihood, and so forth. These obviously are intended to inspire viewers to emulate these standards in their own lives. Television ads are so slick that few people recognize the many hours of hard work and retakes required to give a true-to-life feel to even a single half- or one-minute commercial. If they only knew, perhaps these ads would lose some of their "reality" status. Designed to create perceived wants and needs, such ads seem both a necessity and a potential danger.

Both children and adults can be affected, particularly teenagers and adults who have trouble with self-esteem and peer relationships. Remember, there is an unconscious and unintentional (implicit) aspect to each of us that can significantly affect even our health and welfare. For example, envy for esteemed brands of athletic shoes and other designer apparel can encourage malicious behavior by some juveniles. Also, the portrayal of skinny females as fashion models may foster anorexia in some aspiring young women.

Hollywood and Broadway

Movies, stage plays, soap operas, and so-called reality shows also may portray artificial standards for personal behavior. Hopefully, their audiences will understand this. But have you ever emerged from a movie theater after getting caught up in a captivating film, only to need a bit of time to adjust your senses about what is real? Very young kids also succumb to the magic of such "escapes." But there remains a question of how much of this it takes to twist a youngster's concept of actual reality. This risk seems compounded now that these exposures often pervade much of kids' wakening hours, often for viewing by more mature family members.

Electronic Games

Some people, teenagers included, will claim that these games offer an escape from a dull reality and even a skill-building challenge to their mental acuity. Have you ever seen very young children at a shopping mall entranced with older kids' repeated game plays? Mothers may happily allow it as a source of "harmless" entertainment. The same can occur at home in families with multiple siblings. With many young children exposed for hours to home and mall electronic games, we should wonder how pervasively these distort their perceptions of true reality. This may seem ridiculous—kids certainly must know the difference! But, if true, at what age: three, thirteen, or twenty-three?

Adults may remember the comic books in which the super heroes always triumphed over the villains. Today, it's electronic games where the good guys are targeted, often marked by the reckless zest that the German study mentioned earlier as brutal thrills. Is that reality?

Play is called one of the essentials to healthy child development. But this "play" is not between a child and a machine. It is interpersonal play. At first, this usually is between the baby and a parent, most frequently the mother. As the child grows, play starts to include personal interaction with other youngsters. From this play, the child gradually learns basic lessons about interacting with others.

Enculturation

Motherly care and nurturing extensively have been transferred to significant others and professional caregivers. It therefore seems worthwhile to examine the potential impact of these shifts on the growth, development, and maturation of offspring. The term enculturation is generally reserved for the assimilation of immigrants into a different culture: learning the language and adopting and adapting to the mores of their new environment. America has seen an influx of immigrants, some of whom shared the same culture of origin. Old cultural characteristics often survive in the new country alongside enculturation into the new culture.

Enculturation also has been used to designate various subsets within a country or culture. One of the most interesting of these has been the study of the use of secrets in social life, whether among Masons or teenage girls. Secrets relate to the concept of exclusiveness. This is true whether disclosed only to select members or wielded as weapons to discriminate against targeted others. Don Merten addressed this in his article "Enculturation Into Secrecy Among Junior High School Girls," published in the *Journal of Contemporary Ethnography*. He reported the strategic use of secrets by junior high school girls to shape friendships and enhance social position. This certainly is no surprise to anyone.

But there appears to be a more pervasive, perhaps unintentional, impact of enculturation on the growth and development of children today. It is not necessarily harmful, but it should be recognized for its ubiquity. This is the product of many factors, but stands in stark contrast to cultures in which mothers breast-feed their infants. Breast-feeding provides continuous visual, verbal, and somatic contact between the two. Bottle-feeding, nannies, day-care centers, and multiple others now seem to supply much to most of the nurturing that nature meant for mothers. The true impact seemed unknown and apparently, until now, had gone unstudied. Society had deemed it all to be acceptable, particularly in response to economic times, mothers' preferences, and the uncertain potential for physical or mental health risks.

It becomes apparent that this course of action has had more proponents than opponents. However, as mentioned earlier, a change may be underway. Voices of authority from researchers now urge breast-feeding for its positive health benefits for both mother and child. Not necessarily opposed to working, some mothers still prefer simply to be mothers, disavowing any interest in participating in the equality of women to work and be rewarded as men.

By now, are you curious how some of these forces work together? The next chapter will introduce some things you may never have heard about being human.

CHAPTER SIX

PRODUCTS OF OUR MINDS

Creativity

VALERIE HUNT WROTE, "THE HIGHER level [of the mind] seems to be outside the domain of material reality as we have been able to measure it. The greatest scientists of all time say that their experimentation is guided by mystical, intuitive insight." She quoted Roger Lewin: "When you've discovered the truth in science, it does have the most extraordinary magical quality about it."

Psychoanalysts and behaviorists in Freud's day believed that material rewards were the primary conscious motivation for creativity. However, in their article "Time Pressure and Creativity: Why Time is Not on Your Side" in the *Harvard Business School Working Knowledge,* social psychologists Teresa Amabile and Leslie Perlow disagreed. They demonstrated something called "intrinsic motivation," when creativity excels as the result of activities undertaken for sheer pleasure. Lack of material rewards and not being judged to meet certain criteria seem to free the individual's creative spirit.

In his book *Flow: The Psychology of Optimal Experience,* Mihaly Csikszentmihalyi carried this theory further. He described a state of mind called the "flow state" or "flow experience." Characteristically, this involves total absorption in the particular activity, lack of self-conscious awareness of the event, and later reflection of having been involved in a "peak experience." The exuberant nature of the sensation may help explain why creativity may be pursued despite all manner of obstacles or difficulties. A good reference to this concept about creativity is Howard Gardner's book *Creating Minds: An Anatomy of Creativity As Seen Through the Lives of Freud, Einstein, Picasso, Stravinsky, Eliot, Graham, and Gandhi.*

Achieving Our Potential

Perhaps the term transcendence should be discussed, especially as Joseph Chilton Pearce (2002) seems to define it in his book. Its literal meaning is "climbing or going beyond." Over time, the term has been used in various ways. Theologians apply it to the nonmaterial nature of God. Philosophers consider it a state of mind. Mystics designate it as a nonphysical dimension that is achievable through certain efforts of the mind, such as meditation.

Consider that each evolutionary advance contributed a significant additional *potential* capability for humankind. You might ask whether this process stops at a certain point in time or achievement. Remember, though, that nature continually tries to improve upon itself. Just like the potential energy in a battery never causes a flashlight or motor to perform unless and until it is called upon, full human potential seems limited to its use.

I think Pearce was reminding us that humankind's continued advancement depends not on nature but on each of us, in a society whose worldview seems to discourage it. It is in this context that my book is intended to serve, to help us understand how "the big picture" developed. Then we may realize how our multiple minds and our evolutionary development not only tell us the limits of our individual control but also remind us of the expanse of control each of us *does* have to help achieve humankind's full potential.

Religions historically have emphasized praying. One kind of prayer is submissive, another is thankful. Other kinds involve asking for blessings, guidance, or the granting of wishes. The first two sometimes seem too mechanical, almost devoid of commitment or belief. The others can be selfish if they seek benefits at the expense of others. But any of them can seem to ignore God's relationship with humankind.

The key message in transcendence is climbing or rising above a person's apparent limitations of his or her circumstances. This seems to require a personal recognition and commitment to one's natural potential. Nature prepared each of us to reach and go beyond what we too often accept. In that sense, transcendence is a state of mind. We are what we think and truly believe.

Naturally, this discussion of human potential focuses on the conscious mind. Remember, however, that each of us also has a subconscious mind and a superconscious mind. Those house aspects of us about which we typically are unaware. It seems that the most effective path for tapping those hidden parts of our mind is hypnotic regression. However, meditation and other personal efforts to silence mind chatter and to allow reflection on our individual inner selves seem to work with practice.

The Biology of Transcendence

Bruce Lipton (2005) was one of the first researchers to acknowledge publicly how his work converted him to believe in a higher power. This appears in his book *The Biology of Belief: Unleashing the Power of Consciousness, Matter, and Miracles.* As a cell biologist, he discovered the significance of intelligence even in primitive single-celled organisms. The word "intelligence" is not the equivalent of "intellect," although we sometimes use them interchangeably. In the fourth edition of the *American Heritage College Dictionary*, the first meaning of intelligence is "the capacity to acquire and apply knowledge."

I discussed this in my previous book *Love and Immortality* under the subhead "An Indiscernible God." I said that each of us as human beings seem to be endowed with a unique soul that recognizes the infinite and eternal potential of the divine. Further, that each of us apparently is offered the opportunity to participate in that potential through the way we live our lives. The intelligence with which each creature is endowed facilitates our participation. In subsequent chapters, you will read how our evolutionary system was designed to facilitate growth and development of all creatures. For nonhumans, some environmental conditions may alter that growth and development. But for humans, unlike nonhumans, there exist opportunities for transcendence. Ironically, we are both the source and outcome of that potential. In this sense, transcendence means "to climb or rise beyond our self-perceived limitations." This was not only a part of nature's plan but also requires responsibility and commitment on our part.

Our realization of potential also involves caring for others as you care for yourself. When we focus our minds on the needs of others, we help both them and ourselves. Selfishness is a prison whose bars are the creation our own doing. The good news is that advances in neurobiology, psychology, and child development are paving the way for a brighter future for all of us if we choose to participate.

Intimacy

We are bombarded every waking moment by information and demands from others. This overloads our five senses and our internally initiated thoughts. We virtually have no time to be alone mentally with our inner selves, our higher-level minds. We are conditioned early in life to believe that our five conscious senses reveal the totality of physical reality. It seems unrealistic that our consciousness ever could access any nonphysical dimension of existence.

Nevertheless, there may be times we can sense an elevated state of mind when we achieve our "personal space." We must not feel guilty of depriving another person of our companionship. Personal space means being able to focus our complete attention (awareness, thinking, and feelings) on our inner selves. Creativity seems to manifest itself in this way. Meditation and prayer are other ways to be alone with our inner selves. These provide opportunities to contemplate who we are, where we came from, and why we are here on earth. This approach to being alone with my inner self is also a definition of intimacy. One dictionary definition of intimacy is "Relation to or indicative of one's deepest nature." This is in sharp contrast to our usual use of the term intimacy to mean either a close proximity or an unselfish, loving relationship with another person.

Intuition

Have you ever had an urge to hasten through an intersection as soon as the stoplight turned green but felt an urge to wait and thereby missed colliding with another car? Or the times you feel you knew who was calling before you picked up the telephone? Or places that seemed familiar but you've never before visited? Or hunches that helped you win in card games, at the racetrack, or in team sports? That may have been your intuition manifesting itself.

Intuition has been described as a personal sense or feeling, seeming to come from out of nowhere. It reminds us of something: a warning, a suggestion, or information of some sort. The way intuition manifests itself seems different for different people. Some perceive it visually, some through sounds, some through actual body sensations; some have a déjà vu experience and some have precognitive episodes. Its source is uncharted, although theories abound. At the time intuition happens, not only is it unexpected, but it also seems to carry a degree of conviction. Our first reaction may be to ignore it, but following it seems to bear out its truth. Some persons feel that, like spiritual experiences, intuition should never be used for selfish gain.

Hypnotic Regression

For some time, psychotherapists have induced hypnosis to enable patients to relive a moment from a younger age, often childhood. The intent is to help heal an emotionally traumatic memory. It now appears that this also can help treat certain neuropsychiatric states that may result from subconscious memories of previous lives. An example might be a fear of choking stemming from strangulation in a past life. Hypnotic regression gradually has attained a status of respectability in the medical community, as more therapists are willing to acknowledge their success with it.

Hypnotic regression was mentioned earlier as a means of recalling experiences and emotions from the fetal state. This seems shocking, until one reviews the many uncanny reports verified by relatives of the hypnotized subject. An especially poignant case involved a woman who described an experience her pregnant mother had. Under hypnosis, the daughter sensed her mother having coffee and cookies with the mother's sister. The mother commented wistfully, "I have a strange feeling that I won't see my child grow up." The mother did die a short time later. After the hypnotic regression, the daughter told the aunt to whom the mother had made the comment. The aunt was flabbergasted. "How could you have known that? You hadn't even been born!"

Guilt and Forgiveness

We human beings are prone to making judgments. Sometimes we believe these are justified through our reasoning or rationalization. At times, such conclusions may be hasty and unintentional. "Judgment" used here is not the same as the so-called divine judgment or that rendered in a court of law. Instead, our judgment is a personal belief. It may appear ironclad to other people.

Guilt and forgiveness are closely linked with personal judgment. Both seem related to personally felt emotions. They may involve a composite of emotions. Anger often is involved. Conceivably, the emotions may change over time and be reflected in the concept of forgiveness. Both guilt and forgiveness may be directed at oneself or at others. We may blame ourselves or others for an action or a failure to act. Friends or other third parties may try to dissuade our sense of guilt, hopefully with good intentions. However, we may reject their efforts as intended simply to reduce the harshness of our judgment. Particularly in self-directed guilt, friends' likely objective is self-forgiveness. Guilt and forgiveness may be two of the most challenging products of our minds. They seem to be unique to humankind. Our human nature often seems to consider our attribution of guilt to someone or something as a God-given right. Of course, forgiveness is one of the mandates common to most of the world's religions. Nevertheless, we may find it extremely difficult to comply. Individually, many of us are particularly vulnerable to self-guilt.

We may base our judgments of guilt and forgiveness on limited information. One key aspect of this is involved in self-incrimination of guilt. Despite any conviction that we are fully informed, it is absolutely impossible to know the unknowable. This involves our spirituality and likely will be dismissed by many people. However, it may be the only source of achieving self-forgiveness. Forgiveness of others seems to involve not only our spirituality but also our human traits of empathy and compassion.

We may wonder why some people seem to lack a sense of guilt. Can researchers identify one or more deficits in neurological growth and development and/or environmental factors that contribute to what court judges have called a "lack of remorse"? This appears to involve a neuropathology that usually is not recognizable to anyone other than a trained professional. Perhaps this is why serial killers often avoid identification and apprehension for some time.

Rumination

As illustrated in the preceding section, not all products of our minds are positive. Ruminating is defined as a practice of cattle. They have a means of regurgitating food as a "cud" which they repeatedly and continually chew on. Unfortunately, some people practice this too—revisiting old wounds repeatedly. This seems akin to an inability to forgive, whether the hurt was self-inflicted or caused by others. Remember the constant chatter of the mind, or the concept of never being able to stop thinking? To tell anyone who is plagued by rumination, "Just stop thinking about it," is about as effective as telling someone who is hyperventilating, "Stop gasping for air."

On a personal note, I am guilty of repeatedly wondering whether I could have improved my care of my wife by doing something differently. Our wise son and daughter have a classic saying—a sort of command I should give to my mind—"Don't go there!" This seems to follow a practice that brain researcher Jill Bolton Taylor found effective during recovery from her massive hemorrhagic left-brain stroke. Apparently, the left brain is the information processor for our five senses and maintains dominance over our right brain. By contrast, the right brain focuses on our feeling senses, like empathy and compassion. Taylor literally reconstructed her left-brain self over many years. Amazingly, she found that she could develop some degree of control over her left brain's ruminating behavior. This seems analogous to our son's and daughter's mind instructions, "Don't go there!"

Chronic rumination can be a classic sign of depression. The person experiencing it may not be able to stop his or her negative downward spiral. He or she may fully recognize the impact this is having on his or her physical and mental well-being. But the individual may feel powerless to control it. This may result in a low self-esteem. The person likely will deny a need for professional counseling but this could be imperative.

Thoughts, Beliefs, and Imagination

All three of these terms apply to products of our minds at different times. Conscious memory may be involved in each concept. Another source of information for all three can be the human senses of reality (i.e., vision, touch, taste, smell, and sound). Thereby, the mind seems clearly to distinguish thoughts, beliefs, and imagination. According to Wikipedia, the process of "reasoning" enables the "intellect to mix, match, merge, sift, and sort concepts, perceptions, and experience" to form judgments.

Thoughts are generic in typically being more generalized and fleeting than the other two. Specific thoughts are not necessarily based on perceived reality but may involve past, present, or projected future experiences. Thoughts also usually are less focused than beliefs or imagination. So we speak of thoughts "racing through our heads."

Beliefs are conscious judgments that we hold as indisputable. Beliefs may be created by reasoning, by acceptance as true, or by personal conviction despite established facts. Placebo and nocebo effects are examples of the third kind of belief. Beliefs based upon personal conviction are sometimes termed a person's "worldview."

Imagination is the process of shaping mental images from all sources of awareness (e.g., thoughts, beliefs, conscious memory, and senses). The mind typically can distinguish between imagination and beliefs. However, when encountering voodoo, a victim can translate imagination into a belief. It also must be acknowledged that imagination can be carried to excess in cases of rumination on guilt-laden experiences. There is reason to believe that this behavior can border on psychopathology.

Very young children have vivid imaginations—at least their parents think so. Elsewhere in my book, I mention Tobin Hart's *The Secret Spiritual World of Children*. People who hold fervent worldviews about certain matters sometimes criticize those who willingly contemplate opposing viewpoints as "open-minded." But it seems reasonable that such critics may miss out on opportunities to consider what appears to be beyond the bounds of reality or conceivability. The phrase "think outside the box" seems to be increasingly popular.

Imagination might be related to creativity (e.g., workplace efforts to solve problems and improve productivity or efficiency may ask employees to "blue sky" ideas). As you read earlier, both imagination and creativity are thought to come from higher levels of the mind. A possible differentiation between the two might be that "original" creativity is said to occur in the absence of pressures or rewards, possibly serendipitously.

Valerie Hunt quoted three eminent neurophysiologists, Penfield, Eccles, and Granit. They felt that the abilities inherent in the higher levels of the mind include insight, intuition, imagination, creativity, reasoning, will, intent, decision, and soul.

Have you ever wondered who you *really* are? Check it out in the next chapter.

Chapter Seven

SELF-ESTEEM

Who Do You Think You Are?

THIS MAY BE THE MOST personally threatening part of this book. As was said earlier, most of us probably feel reasonably comfortable with the individuals we *assume* we are. Most of us self-consciously may not spend much time contemplating our positive attributes. But researchers say that we typically replay our self-perceived deficiencies to extreme. We all want to feel good about ourselves, self-confident, proud, content, and successful. We want to avoid feeling ashamed, guilty, or inferior. So we spend our lives trying to sustain the former and negate the latter, sometimes at whatever cost to ourselves or to others.

It appears that self-esteem exists in both implicit and explicit states of memory. Explicit self-esteem apparently develops after implicit self-esteem. The former is facilitated when a child self-consciously becomes aware of his or her perceived standing among family members, peers, and significant others. The young person then likely will implement behavior to support or improve his or her felt reputation or position. This could justify a higher explicit self-esteem.

Implicit Self-Esteem

It is only natural for adults to think that their interactions with, and behavior around, babies is harmless to those infants. Just be concerned about the safety, nutrition, and comfort of the very young, they are told.

But you've read examples, often with lifelong implications, that suggest that the opposite is true.

Newcomers approach the world in an innocent, trusting manner. Perhaps as an extension of their animal instincts, they need to appraise their world as a safe or threatening place. Infants sense and unconsciously accept as trustworthy and authoritative those experiences and emotions represented by the words, behavior, and interactions of persons closest to them. During the very early years of a child's life, however, the non-verbal behavior of parents and caregivers often sends the child conflicting messages of approval or disapproval. These may be unconsciously or unintentionally sent. To the very young, however, these messages sometimes are very confusing.

Nevertheless, the composite of these imprinted implicit memories can be considered the offspring's implicit self-esteem: what the child unquestionably accepts as his or her "self." For the rest of his or her life, the newcomer will unconsciously carry a personally unassailable set of attitudes and beliefs about him- or herself. Whether negative or positive, the child can neither remember nor intentionally assess or address this implicit self-esteem with traditional psychological methods. Moreover, to challenge these beliefs might provoke intolerable tensions between implicit and explicit self-esteem.

Explicit Self-Esteem

By contrast, our conscious self-beliefs constitute our explicit self-esteem, of which we continually are reminded, sometimes painfully. But our implicit memory system *unconsciously and unintentionally* controls our behavioral responses to other people, circumstances, and things. That memory also is an immutable force in our *unconscious self-appraisal* or implicit self-esteem.

Researchers have studied the relationship between implicit and explicit self-esteems. Most feel that the two are distinctly separate systems, like implicit and explicit memory. The former exists a couple of years before the latter emerges. Explicit self-esteem depends upon a child becoming aware of his or her perceived standing among family members, peers, and significant others. The young person likely will implement behavior to support or improve his or her reputation or position and thus justify a higher explicit self-esteem. Studies have shown that a person's implicit self-esteem may vary widely from his or her explicit self-esteem.

Apparently, the eventual development of explicit memory is related to verbal ability and cognition. Cognition is the mental process of knowing, including aspects such as awareness, perception, reasoning, and judgment. Cognition therefore stimulates and facilitates exchanges between people and enables one's conscious realization of self (explicit self-esteem).

It has been proposed that certain dimensions of explicit self-esteem, if reinforced often enough, may become internalized. This conceivably might have the potential of affecting implicit self-esteem. This was one finding of Tracy DeHart and colleagues in their publication "What Lies Beneath: Parenting Style and Implicit Self-Esteem" in the *Journal of Social Psychology*. Different styles of parenting seem to vary in their effect on implicit and explicit self-esteem. For example, over-protectiveness may improve implicit self-esteem in the very young. But it could be a negative for explicit self-esteem as children age and try to develop independent identities.

This led DeHart to believe that implicit self-esteem is more affected by the nature of an infant's interactions with the mother. However, explicit self-esteem is more dependent on later experiences with peers and significant others. Some mental health professionals seem to believe that a high implicit self-esteem makes children more resilient to life's exigencies. Some researchers have linked high explicit and low implicit self-esteem with greater defensiveness and higher levels of narcissism.

Narcissism

Narcissism is sometimes called "narcissistic personality disorder." This is characterized by a display of self-importance or self-centeredness, often extreme. Researchers have suggested that narcissists' mindset and behavior may reflect an effort greater than normal to boost their explicit self-esteem. Apparently, this may be related to an unconsciously low implicit self-esteem. If so, this seems to help validate the significance of implicit memory in shaping unconscious and unintentional behavior later in life.

Other traits of narcissism include

- an inability to empathize with others,
- a need to be controlling and the center of attention,
- expectations for admiration and affection,
- entitlement without making a contribution.

Some mental health professionals feel that narcissism is more characteristic of the adolescent than of the adult. Perhaps this results from the adolescent's eventually confronting the realities of life and accommodating to them.

Self-Love

Self-love may seem hedonistic and self-centered. But think about it. If I don't respect and admire myself for the unique individual I am, if I don't forgive myself for my unintentional acts that harmed others, if my inner self doesn't regard me with esteem and value, then how can I possibly love others? Our love for others should be selfless, considering each soul a unique creation. Others deserve the respect, compassion, and consideration that we would want from them. Love of self after love of God seems imperative as a precursor to loving others. But self-love has many dimensions. The Western culture's emphasis on *explicit* self-esteem in child development programs appears aimed at developing one's image rather than one's character. It's like I'm too preoccupied with my own misery to make room to love others.

Once I'm comfortable with my own self-image, loving others should not threaten my ego. Without positive self-esteem, my ego rides the turbulent currents of others' behavior toward me. I sometimes need to protect it by depending on the masks of power, wealth, or status. But just imagine someone with not only a fragile explicit self-esteem but also a shaky implicit self-esteem. Suppose his or her early years were filled with degrading personal experiences—a double dose of trouble!

A Healthy Self-Esteem

This seems to emphasize the need for developing a healthy self-esteem (both implicit and explicit). Parents can encourage this through a balance between authoritarianism and permissiveness. Admittedly, this can be difficult. Consider the ancestral influences on the parents and the mores of today's society. Perhaps the bottom line here for parents is threefold:

• loving attention, support, and continuing reassurance
• establishing mutually acceptable guidelines
• continuing personal interaction conducive to trust and to resolution of problems

Remember that babies enter this world eager to learn about themselves and their environment. Their personal encounters with others seem to form a backbone of impressions, from fetus through early years. Much of this foundation seems to depend on their experiences: first with the mother for nine months, then with both parents and other family members, and eventually with other caregivers. Then, probably for the rest of the child's life, he or she consciously will try to sustain and improve his or her self-image—as he or she perceives it to appear to others.

Explicit self-esteem therefore is a very self-conscious part of us. It can be tested psychologically. Testing of implicit self-esteem is much less reliable, for good reason. Each of us creates his or her own individual conscious self-image or explicit self-esteem. It is subject to many experiences and emotions as well as to our continuing efforts to improve it. It is shaped by our personal feelings about how we compare to others and to others' expectations of us.

The latter influence—others' expectations of us—can powerfully affect our explicit self-esteem, whether the others are parents or peers. For example, there seems to be incessant pressure by some parents for their children to excel in sports, business, or entertainment fields. This sometimes seems to reflect parents' desires vicariously to enjoy rewards they personally have failed to achieve. Parents also may literally require their children to pursue careers or marriages that maintain or enhance family status. Peer expectations may be more accurately termed "peer challenges." Some are imagined and some are implied or verbalized by peers.

Explicit self-esteem seems most susceptible to family and peer influences in pre-teens and teenagers. This is when children have achieved a measure of understanding and decision-making ability. But a child's judgment and conduct often succumb to irrationality in the face of such influences. Puberty seems to promote battle lines drawn between parents and children. Instinctive desires for independence build upon greater time spent with peers than with parents. Perhaps one of the greatest challenges facing young people today could be the tug-of-war that might rage between their explicit and implicit self-esteems. Pre-teens and teenagers sometimes desperately seek acceptance, status, and even love that may have been missing from their earlier lives.

Some approaches to therapy offer programs to raise explicit self-esteem. An emphasis on early nurturing of a positive self-image seems rational, to foster a favorable self-worth. This should enhance one's ability to interact favorably with others and to confront the multitude of life challenges. Jack Canfield and Harold C. Well's book *100 Ways to Enhance Self-Concept in the Classroom* could be worthwhile reading for teachers.

But two problems seem to persist. First, this necessarily seems to address only explicit self-esteem. It cannot address the typically hidden implicit self-esteem and thus might cause potential conflicts between the two. Second, enhancing explicit self-esteem may foster self-aggrandizement. This could be especially true for those who continue to feel unfulfilled due to conflicts with their implicit self-image.

Some people consider self-esteem as a trait to be earned, a form of self-confidence. However, in his Web article "Raising Self-Esteem and Reducing Self-Defeating Shame (Hedonistic Disinhibition)," Bryce Kaye seems to disagree. He writes that, most often, self-esteem is part of an individual's unconscious (implicit) perceptions of "felt deservingness or undeservingness (core shame)." He suggests that a treatment called "hedonic disinhibition" can positively improve self-esteem, "removing underlying emotional blocks to happiness in a person's unconscious."

Conflicts between the Two Self-Esteems

Sigmund Freud claimed that psychopathology arises from conflict at the unconscious level and can be regulated if the source is confronted consciously. But researchers report difficulty even in having subjects self-assess their explicit self-esteem. One reason seems to be a natural tendency to inflate their perceptions of themselves. Accurate self-assessment seems improbable for implicit self-esteem. Yet some psychologists have found that responses to certain word-picture associations reveal implicit influences, such as family or group ethnic prejudice.

Don't forget that, lying hidden just below self-awareness is the ubiquitous influence of implicit self-esteem. Some neuroscientists and psychologists now seem to view the potential tension between explicit and implicit self-esteem as a significant factor in some mental illnesses. An article by Thomas Fuchs in the medical journal *Current Opinion in Psychiatry* indicts implicit memory as "the link between deficient early interaction experiences, dysfunctional bonding patterns, and disturbed affect regulations, which play a decisive role in most mental disorders."

The Lure of Competition

We are a competitive society. But some groups try to level the playing field by declaring no winners or losers and awarding trophies to all participants. Which raises the question, how natural is this? Is it an artificial attempt to disallow the growth of innate responsibility, deserved reward, and character? Does it thwart the growth and development of a child and the subsequent adult's ability to cope with life off the playing field?

To maintain positive explicit self-esteem, we sometimes set goals, for ourselves or for our groups, related to tasks, progress, or achievements. These include sporting matches and advances at work. How good we feel afterward seems directly proportional to how well we excel. In contrast, if we fail, our despondency may know no limits. After all, we may have spent many years reinforcing our perceived beliefs about ourselves, with persistent efforts to improve our felt standing. There may be obvious measures we accept as gospel truth. These include our bodily appearance, the color of our skin, our intellectual or competitive achievements, and so forth. We compare ourselves to others, most often *without fully knowing others' actual standing or their true appraisals of us.*

Human ego survival almost necessitates that we avoid complimenting others, except loved ones. Even then, as between spouses, the desire for power may prevail. It almost seems sacrificial to one's ego to sincerely acknowledge another person's excelling. But we usually seem oblivious to these facts in our constant drive to outshine one another. However, competition is a learned skill. It involves much more than winning or losing. Beliefs and attitudes children adopt about competition can significantly influence not only their lives but also the lives of others they encounter throughout adulthood.

Young children do not have an innate competitive nature. Many people would deny this when watching kids interact. What they do have is a natural love of play. Play has been called one of the essential ingredients of a healthy childhood. Researchers stress that opportunity for play should be encouraged in early infancy. Play between mother and baby fosters the intimacy nature intended. Only after they reach about five years of age do children begin to compete and compare their skills with those of other children. One way of thinking about this stage is that now "play" simply offers more challenges and potential rewards. About then, children are really into using their five physical senses. They enjoy being the center of attention and receiving constant reassurance through praise and admiration. They start to "want to do it myself!" They enjoy simple games, played for fun or for play's sake. These are games in which being the winner carries a momentary pleasure and being the loser becomes a stimulus to repeat the game. Gloating or disillusionment is not an innate feeling at that age.

Children must be ten or eleven before they can function well as team members and handle defeat gracefully. They characteristically become more achievement oriented at this age and try to please significant others. But they demand to be treated as individuals and to be kept informed. About then, frustration starts to emerge about tasks, independent decision making, and restrictions or discipline. Their desire to please parents and significant others may conflict with their innermost attitudes toward competition itself or toward the kinds of events in which they are encouraged to participate. Rebellion or grudging participation may occur. This is an age at which peer, group, or even gang membership and approval can become appealing.

Inherent in developing a healthy competitive lifestyle is consideration of a child's natural temperament. Some thrive on competition while others fear it, possibly due to parental and other environmental factors earlier in infancy. Healthy competitiveness obviously involves skills and helps develop quick decision making, self-control, discipline, coordination, problem solving, self-confidence, and maturity. But every competitive match, in sports, business, or personal life likely will result in an individual or a team winning. How the other person or team handles the outcome is a mark of his, her, or their resilience. To paraphrase a statement made elsewhere in this book, "We often forget our wins to drown in despair over our losses."

Shame and Humiliation

A person's comfort level for social interaction is not easily visible to others, and it may vary depending on the situation. The nature of that comfort level conceivably may have its roots in both implicit and explicit memory. One extreme example is something psychologists call "social anxiety disorder" or "social phobia." Christopher Lane discussed this in his book *Shyness: How Normal Behavior Became a Sickness.* He argues that the diagnosis of social anxiety disorder has become too broad, with medication being prescribed when the patients are not "chronically impaired."

Despite Lane's belief, psychiatrists acknowledge that the disorder can exist and is difficult to distinguish from normal shyness. Persons with social anxiety may appear gregarious and outgoing at times, especially in situations in which their comfort level is not challenged. Experts claim that this condition is characterized by an internal fear of being humiliated or negatively judged by other people. This leads sufferers to limit their exposure in potentially embarrassing social situations.

Shame can be learned with explicit memory, after a child reaches an age of conscious awareness and comprehension, typically age three or four. Earlier, a child can unconsciously store embarrassment and shame in implicit memory, with its accompanying emotions. This might be particularly difficult to diagnose due to its unconscious and unintentional behavioral response imprints. Fear of shame and humiliation obviously can be instilled by life experiences from birth through early teenage years. It can be an almost insurmountable tension between implicit and explicit self-esteems, as young people try to build their self-confidence and independence. This can be particularly prominent as they encounter increasing numbers of previously unfamiliar people as they grow older.

Throughout this book, you will find the recurring themes of love and healthy, unselfish self-love. Authorities on child development and mental health seem unanimous in their emphasis on these as essential building blocks for a healthy lifestyle. Also, healthy self-respect and self-love seem to require loving support and reassurance from parents and significant others throughout childhood. This can reach into the time in early adulthood when the prefrontal cortex or "moderator brain" finishes maturing.

The risks and potential pitfalls facing caregivers are beyond numbering, and negative results are readily evident in our society today. Depending on the circumstances that led to experiences of shame and humiliation, some authorities say that these can precipitate anger, rage, and even violence later in life.

Positive Self-Esteem

Perhaps surprisingly, true explicit self-esteem seems to grow in direct proportion to our efforts and satisfactions in helping others. It also might help outweigh negative *implicit* self-esteem we acquired in our very early years. The personal satisfaction of caring for and helping others seems to offer a conscious sense of well-being, contentment, and even happiness. This then becomes conducive to a positive *explicit* self-image—a version of self-esteem necessarily inaccessible from hedonistic self-love.

Another avenue to positive self-esteem involves interpersonal relations, instead of achievements in the entertainment, business, or sports worlds. This involves the affirmative gut feeling each of us yearns for: of being respected, valued, and appreciated. It stems from affections on both sides, perhaps like reciprocal acceptance, understanding, respect, and acknowledgment. It is a sort of variant of love. It rewards each participant with his or her unconditional emotional contribution. It is not something that can be turned on by willpower alone. It is a personal investment in the other person, but without anticipation of anything more in return than is contributed to the relationship. This waxes very philosophical, doesn't it? But it truly is reflected in what we call empathy, as native Americans used to say, "a willingness to walk in another's moccasins for a moon."

A third approach to positive self-esteem was portrayed in the book *I'm OK; You're OK*, written by navy psychiatrist Thomas Harris over twenty-five years ago. Basic to the concepts offered by Harris was a combination of assessments of yourself and others, with the eventual goal of feeling "I'm OK; you're OK." Obviously, this involved whether you felt accepted by others, self-confident, valued, loved, appreciated, secure, competent, understood, and content, and had an overall positive self-image. The same parameters were used to determine your attitude toward others.

Influence of Personal Dissatisfaction

There seems to be a rampant growth of divergence between what might be termed "the haves" and "the have-nots." Although economic, ethnic, and environmental factors may contribute to this, the situation seems more deep-seated and far-reaching. The distinction here seems most apparent in the gap between young people's self-image and their expectations. It may have started years ago and manifests itself even in some of us as adults. On one hand, we find some teenagers reaching out to peers and older strangers for emotional support that they perceived was missing from close family and friends. Their behavior often seeks to fill needs to build self-image and self-confidence, sometimes regardless of costs. On the other hand, we find some teenagers so bursting with narcissism that "the world is their oyster." Nothing appears to be out of reach for their self-perceived abilities as well as their expectations for recognition and reward. The two opposing scenarios pose a fascinating question of how young people can be so different. Personally, I wonder if radically different childhood environments shaped their implicit self-esteems.

Today's Youth: What Some Researchers Are Saying

Young people's unrealistic appraisal of possible outcomes and their compromise of common sense seem to be major factors in two widespread behaviors: the use of illegal substances and childbirths by unwed teenagers. If the present state of affairs is any measure, we appear to be encouraging greedy, egocentric, and careless behavior in society. Some observers claim that the inward focus on conscious self-appreciation may further promote intolerance, entitlement, victimhood, and narcissism. Tolerance risks non-judgmental acceptance of others. Ironically, we may disavow for ourselves standards we set for others. Beliefs of entitlement, rampant in today's society, evoke insistent feelings of deserving benefits that exceed our personal contributions. Ironically, this does not seem restricted to economic, educational, or ethnic backgrounds. It poses the question of whether society itself has fostered this.

Columnist Anthony Robinson issued a challenge in "Articles of Faith: The Unfortunate Age of Entitlement in America." Self-esteem is important, but now self-esteem "seems to have morphed into entitlement." There seems to be a narrow ledge of self-perception that, on one side, risks true honesty and, on the other, becomes the ultimate selfishness. The current mood seems to be a "culture of complaint," he feels. "We have," he observes, developed a prevailing attitude of "blame, complaint and grievance." Moreover, we've totally forgotten the value of saying *please, thank you*, and *I'm sorry*. He concludes, "Entitlement is the handmaiden of the ego, the sign of a neglected, malnourished soul." Robinson sees a dismal forecast for America if this persists. "In the end, it's the entitled who, however rich, are truly poor. Instead of knowing life as a gift, life turns into something that's taken for granted—or worse, begrudged. That's real poverty, and no sense of entitlement can alleviate it."

After examining 1.3 million personality surveys over the past twenty-five years, Jean Twenge and fellow researchers concluded that the present generation is the most self-centered in history. In her book *Generation Me: Why Today's Young Americans are More Confident, Assertive, Entitled—and More Miserable Than Ever Before*, Twenge looked at generational differences in self-esteem, individualism, anxiety, and sexuality. This new self-centered mentality encourages higher explicit self-esteem but also can produce higher levels of anxiety, cynicism, and loneliness, she said. It seems reasonable that information overload, mentioned earlier, might have created unrealistic expectations for life. This could prompt dissatisfaction and cynicism about personal experiences that provide anything less than what German researchers called brutal thrill stimuli. Might this mindset push teenagers to or over the brink of disaster or violence as their hormones surge in puberty and they experiment with high-risk behavior?

Tied in with attitudes of intolerance and entitlement is the ubiquitous idea of victimhood, placing the blame for personal inadequacies elsewhere. Legal defenses of criminal actions increasingly seem to employ this approach and compassionate judges and juries may accept it. It is flagrant disregard of personal accountability for the accused.

Related to this is the apparent phenomenon of treating behavioral problems as diseases, amenable to counseling and drug therapy. All of this seems to border on shifting from the responsibility for self-control to accepting self-indulgence. Some researchers have blamed this as narcissistic in nature, in a sense promoting success rather than self-respect. It seems to amount to putting oneself on a pedestal, in disregard of reality. It could lead to personal expectations for undeserved recognition and self-appeasement, as well as a loss of respect for others.

A Personal Experience: Parents

Let me insert here a personal experience. For six months in the 1970s, I worked almost full time for the Indianapolis Task Force on Drug Abuse. Sadly, I found that parental attitudes that existed then still persist today. "Not my child!" was the insistence I heard from families who apparently viewed their public image more important than acceptance of responsibility and the needs of their offspring. In this case, the word "needs" does not include shielding their children from acknowledging accountability, as many parents seem to do. This left me worried that their children's take-away perceptions of their parents' denial would somehow reinforce the children's view that "anything goes." But it also reminded me that the children's behavior might have been a desperate cry for attention, even love. Denial of accountability seems a poor substitute for love. Today, I would attribute such children's views of the world and of themselves as possible millstones perpetuating lifelong behavior.

Who Are You ... Really?

Implicit self-esteem is a powerful, but mostly unrecognized, influence. As part of implicit memory, it was shaped when we were very young. It constitutes the self that we tacitly acknowledge must be the real us, since it was built from words and actions of those whom we considered authority figures. On one hand, we may have been smothered in loving, caring feedback that set us on a pedestal. On the other, we may have been criticized constantly as worthless and inconsiderate. There seems to be an obvious question: if my implicit memory imprinted an indisputable self-image of me, where does my explicit self-esteem fit into the picture. Are there continuing unrealized tensions between my implicit self-esteem and my explicit self-esteem? In other words, are my efforts to improve my explicit self-esteem related to my unconscious implicit self-esteem? Are these some of the tensions that researchers now implicate in mental illnesses?

Each of us has other characteristic dimensions that shape our lives. Some of these are apparent to other people. Only we are aware of some of them. There are still others that even we don't recognize. We'll explore this variegated landscape in the next chapter.

CHAPTER EIGHT

THE REAL YOU

Behavior: The Visible You

YOU MAY AGREE THAT A person's behavior, as demonstrated in a variety of challenging encounters with other people, problems, and circumstances, could possibly be the litmus test of resilience (resilience will be discussed later). This sometimes may be reflected in an individual's personality. It naturally could involve his or her explicit self-esteem. But it also depends on his or her implicit programmed behavioral responses, which are visible measures of the invisible implicit memory and implicit self-esteem. Humans can camouflage their behavior, as exemplified by actors and actresses, and as differentiated between mechanical and actual caring and love. Perhaps babies can distinguish between the two when interacting with a caregiver; spouses no doubt recognize the difference with each other.

Perhaps one of the most visible demonstrations of extreme reactive behavior is so-called road rage. Many researchers point to self-esteem as a root cause, as it relates to suddenly being confronted by a totally unexpected perceived affront. Other examples of reactive behavior might include revenge of a jealous lover or spouse or killing by a defrauded drug dealer. Of course, road rage is usually impulsive; revenge may be premeditated. The word "affront" is used deliberately. Anything that threatens our self-esteem must be dealt with. It's human nature. When something is consciously recognizable as such, our emotional responses kick in. But if we don't consciously recognize it as a threat, our reaction may come from our deep-seated implicit (unconscious) self-esteem and our conditioned emotional responses. For example, if our implicit self-esteem bears the scars of continually being belittled by parents and siblings at an early age, this may undermine our explicit self-esteem, however robust the latter may appear to be. For cheating spouses, illicit lovers, and defaulting drug users, the risk is obvious. For victims of road rage, the result is totally unexpected, unless the victim initiated the reaction by conducting him- or herself in an improper, illegal, or defiant driving maneuver.

To help explain these points, the following conclusions were distilled from various Web sites about the conventional thinking regarding road rage and other spontaneous eruptions of emotions. Researchers point to at least two symptoms: a feeling of rage and a desire to punish. Anger can be a stimulating feeling. In a sense, it is somewhat akin to sensing physical danger and reacting accordingly. Defending oneself always has been regarded as acceptable. Venting anger has been likened to a catharsis and was traditionally preferable to being bottled up, for emotional stability. Now it is recognized as creating stress, with a negative impact on health.

Deborah Tannen characterized such emotional outbursts as a visible indication of how "contentious" our society has become, in her *Washington Post* article "For Argument's Sake: Why Do We Feel Compelled to Fight About Everything?" Disputes and disagreements pop up often in interpersonal relationships, at home, in the office, and on the sports field. Tannen called these examples of what she termed our "culture of disrespect in everyday life." Some result in expressions of extreme violence, like road rage and revenge killings. Some researchers define these actions as a "lack of self-restraint." But consider what you have read about implicit memory and implicit self-esteem. It seems implausible that these outbursts might *not* also reflect tensions between implicit and explicit self-esteems.

Admittedly, such impulsive actions seem exacerbated by pressures of modern life. Attempts to travel are horrendous in the milieu of never-ending congestion and delays, and the press of competition. Continuing press coverage of militant ways to avenge some perceived slight or injustice leads to copycat events. Simply feeling in control of the most powerful potential instruments of aggression ever developed must convey an unparalleled sense of power.

Then, too, there is the so-called style of driving, either developed through procedural learning from aggressive mentors or adopted over time as ways to be more assertive and competitive. Most drivers would defend such behavior as legitimate in today's environment. Still, it often borders on recklessness and often disrespects other drivers' presence on the road. One example was a young woman apparently in a rush and frustrated by the lack of speed of the car in front of her. So she proceeded to block the other car and yank the other, older woman driver, from her car and beat her unmercifully. What is worse, gunshots have become so frequent on highways that they often don't make news.

At least one researcher tied road rage to self-esteem, according to the perceived meaning that an offended driver attaches to the event. Possibly feeling insulted, demeaned, wronged, disrespected, or deprived of achieving a legitimate goal, we retaliate. Our emotions overwhelm our good judgment and disregard the possible consequences.

The contrasting viewpoint and response would require us to sacrifice control of the situation. We would have to admit that the other driver's action might have had a valid reason. We then could back off and relinquish ownership of the occasion to the other person. This likely would only happen reluctantly and probably inexplicably for us.

We never seem able to travel from setting to setting without emotional baggage from unresolved issues. An argument with our spouse before leaving for work, a criticism from our boss or an envied promotion of a fellow employee, the inability to close an anticipated deal, or even just a menacing or mocking grin on someone's face may haunt us incessantly.

The American Automobile Association defines our cars as extensions of our territory, and it stresses that our instinctual urge is to protect our territory. Any action by another car that threatens control of our territory represents aggression and must be dealt with accordingly. We may feel that horn sounds are insufficient. If our emotional baggage is overwhelming, we may feel we must deal a more severe reminder to the offending driver. Whatever the cause, road rage, revenge killings, and similar happenings continue to punctuate our land. Few, if any, measures short of emotional restraint and self-revelation seem likely to improve our visible side.

Beliefs: The Invisible You

We typically use various terms to designate the part of us that we may claim is responsible for our behavior, such as moods, attitudes, feelings, emotions, or beliefs. These stand in sharp contrast to such mental constructs as ideas, plans, concepts, intentions, and actions. In a sense, the former terms color or shade the latter—they add the personal touch that is uniquely ours. I use the expression "may claim" intentionally. Sigmund Freud spoke of our conscious and unconscious minds. It seems that the word "beliefs" captures the more specific, persistent, and uniquely individual aspects of both minds, one conscious, one unconscious. Later, we'll examine the spectrum of emotions that help mediate beliefs in both minds.

Ever think that saying "thank you" could change your life? Many people will probably shrug this off as just some more meaningless drivel meant to sell millions of self-help books. But scientists are now finding that Norman Vincent Peale's *The Power of Positive Thinking*, first published in 1952, was right on target all along. The October 2007 issue of *Reader's Digest* had a condensed version of researchers' discoveries described by Deborah Norville in her book *Thank You Power: Making the Science of Gratitude Work for You*. Amazingly, by just being perceptive of and grateful for small things on a regular basis, we can improve both our mental and physical health as well as our relationships with others.

Robert Emmons, professor of psychology at the University of California at Davis, is a leader in this relatively new field of positive psychology. His research, along with that of Michael McCullough, produced a book for health professionals called *The Psychology of Gratitude (Series in Affective Science)*. Emmons' more recent book, *Thanks! How the New Science of Gratitude Can Make You Happier*, was written to help share the positive benefits with all of us. Interestingly, positive thinking stimulates positive action and somehow involves human energy fields.

Gary Schwartz (2007) and colleagues added credence to the existence of human energy fields and their potential value in healing in their book *The Energy Healing Experiments: Science Reveals Our Natural Power to Heal*. His research also revealed the significance of conscious intention. Melvin Morse told of a six-year-old dying from a neuroblastoma. The youngster had other ideas. Following a very vivid dream, he drew a picture of himself without the tumor. He had a complete remission. Apparently, he and others like him who had what were termed "spontaneous remissions" had not yet learned that miracles are generally considered impossible.

The Institute of Noetic Sciences published a bibliography by O'Regan and Hirschberg of all scientifically recorded cases of so-called miracle cures. Although these are usually thought to be rare, many, if not most, types of illnesses have exhibited spontaneous remissions in a surprisingly significant number of cases. These even include some malignancies, such as skin and genitourinary cancers.

In their book *The Placebo Response: How You Can Release the Body's Inner Pharmacy for Better Health,* Harold and Daralyn Brody described a classic case of mind over body involving a terminally ill cancer patient and an experience called the placebo effect. This occurred years ago and involved the experimental drug Krebiozen. The patient's physician reluctantly agreed to give him the drug, then was surprised to note the patient's remarkable response. As the news media loudly decried the drug as ineffective, the patient's condition deteriorated. His doctor gave him another treatment, but assured him it was a new, improved Krebiozen. The patient's response again was amazingly positive, but when the Food and Drug Administration announced conclusively that Krebiozen was not effective, the patient's condition rapidly worsened, and he soon died.

Another case of mind over body, but with different results, is referred to as the nocebo effect. Bruce Lipton (2005) cited a classic example. This was depicted in the Discovery Health Channel's 2003 program, *Placebo: Mind Over Medicine.* It involved a Nashville, Tennessee, physician and his patient, who was told he had cancer of the esophagus in 1974. At the time, this was considered by all to be 100 percent fatal. The patient was treated but died within a few weeks after his diagnosis. Surprisingly, an autopsy discovered that there was very little cancer in his body, definitely not enough to kill him. These two illustrations emphasize how our beliefs can dramatically affect our health, indeed our very lives. Henry Ford was quoted as saying, "If you believe you can or if you believe you can't—you're right."

Primitive instincts include growth and protection of the individual. When protective instincts kick in—fight or flight—energy is diverted from growth. Translated to our modern-day lives, certain stresses can restrict the ability of our bodies to perform well. Obviously, this depends on the intensity and persistence of the stress. But we are reminded that it is important not only to remove stressors, but also to live joyful, loving, and fulfilling lives that encourage growth processes.

We hardly ever hear the word "passion" used today. Obviously, it has some negative connotations. But in the context of meaning "a strong or intense interest or enthusiasm," it can represent a particular goal or objective. Unfortunately, to many of us, our world often appears jaded. Perhaps it's because some countries have been flooded with every imaginable convenience. When it comes to food, health care, housing, and even transportation, we all too often insist on personal entitlement and disavow personal responsibility. Despite outcries demanding justice, there is public antipathy against the rule of law, even to the extent of blackballing those who help police catch criminals. Remnants remain of ethnic disfavor. Equal and individual opportunity seems less encouraged.

But, every so often, someone who portrays an unrivaled passion will appear on the world stage. It may be an artist, a benefactor, a sports figure, or any other individual who seeks to excel in achievement and share with others. In doing so, he or she makes the world a better place for everyone. It reminds us that passion is not totally outmoded. But this would seem to exclude those whose motivation is selfish, solely for personal gain—for wealth, power, or politics. On perhaps on a more modest scale, passion is said to be necessary for the full actualization of human potential. Ever asked someone what his or her passion in life was and gotten a nonsensical stare? By contrast, have you ever met anyone who seems to love life: his or her work, relationships with others, time for relaxation, and appreciation of the outdoors? Could it be because he or she has a passion for life?

There was a news report about an Australian physician who seemed able successfully to treat eating disorders in teenage girls by helping them identify a passion in life. It seems that getting the girls to focus on a personally rewarding pursuit gave their lives a more meaningful goal. Consequently, it dissuaded them from habitually dwelling on whatever was driving their eating disorder.

The Biology of Beliefs

Humankind long has thought that genes are the links between generations. Genes supposedly determine inherited traits and literally foretell the health and well-being of succeeding offspring. But recent research has shown that genes are simply "molecular blueprints" to guide cellular development and production, and ultimately to produce tissues and organs. Cell biologist Bruce Lipton provided a breakthrough understanding of the intricate functions of what he calls the "smart cell." Amazingly, each cell has an ability to "read" its environment and apply these "signals" to genetic blueprints, to control growth and development. You may find this plausible. But you may find it more difficult to accept that these signals from the cell's environment can be significantly influenced by our personal thoughts and beliefs!

Lipton's book (2005) aptly is subtitled *Unleashing the Power of Consciousness, Matter, and Miracles.* It details Lipton's path from being a medical school professor teaching traditional dogma about genes to becoming a groundbreaking researcher. He devoted himself to finding the true, but limited, role that genes play in human growth and development. My book will highlight a few of his findings. These apply to the central theme of how memory—particularly implicit memory of mother and baby—can be involved in human growth and development, both physical and mental.

The environment of a cell naturally does not mean the surroundings outside the human body. For example, the environment of a pancreatic cell is its location in that gland. But just as our minds continually sense signals from our immediate surroundings, we also receive information from across the earth and space. Obviously, the latter information transfer involves such things as wireless signals. Similarly, our bodies depend on multiple biological systems to move information from place to place, a variety of "messengers." Some even seem to have an almost immediate effect.

In pregnancy, at least two environments are involved: the fetal womb and the mother's surroundings. Research has demonstrated that the fetus is sensitive to happenings in the mother's environment and to her conscious reaction to those events. It even seems reasonable that the fetus also could be sensitive to the mother's unconscious conditioned response guided by her implicit memory. It may seem to stretch credibility, but the fetus has been shown to be aware of any debate between mother and father about wanting the child. This can imprint in the fetus' implicit memory. If the mother's implicit memory holds a stringent prohibition of abortion, the fetus might even detect her refusal to have an abortion. The potential impact of this revelation upon the child is discussed elsewhere in this book.

It seems widely accepted that mothers who adhere to proper obstetrical care and refrain from detrimental influences have better chances for healthy babies. It also is a fact that various products besides blood, antibodies, and nutrients pass across the placenta to the fetus. Yet, mothers less often realize that a number of biochemicals produced by their bodies also are transferred to their fetuses. For example, if the mother-to-be is employed in a very stressful setting, her body may increase levels of hormones specifically to help her cope. These substances, such as adrenalin, are part of the fight-or-flight instinctual mechanisms. Part of their action is to divert blood away from the brain and digestive tract to muscles. This shunting has the capacity adversely to affect other parts of the body that depend upon a regular blood supply for growth and development. As these hormones cross the placenta, they can have the same negative effect on the fetus. Extend this to imagine the potential impact of repeated or sustained higher levels of these biochemicals. It is increasingly evident that even our unconscious behavior and conscious thoughts can influence fetal growth and development in many ways.

It has been said that we downloaded without question most of our fundamental behaviors into our subconscious mind in our early years by observing other people. As we are involved in interpersonal encounters later in life, our automatic (implicit) responses often determine our behavior. This is especially true if our conscious (explicit) mind is concerned with other distractions. Only when we self-consciously focus our intentions and reason our behavior can we fully expect our thoughts to exert their maximum beneficial effects on our well-being.

Psychological or neurological problems can occur if tensions develop between our subconscious programs and our conscious will. Some psychologists have always emphasized that the treatment of mental health disorders should take into account the influence of implicit memory. It is not hard to imagine how implicit behavioral responses might be involved in such conditions as bipolar disorder, depression, or even schizophrenia. For example, some mental health professionals now feel that mood swings in bipolar disorder may result from problems involving the unconscious and conscious control of emotions.

False Beliefs

Remember that procedural memory is like learning to drive a car. You automatically can drive without being able to remember when or in what context you learned: the details of the time, place, and teacher when you were taught. Now, two researchers have an explanation. In their book *Welcome to Your Brain: Why You Lose Your Car Keys but Never Forget How to Drive and Other Puzzles of Everyday Life,* researchers Sandra Aamodt and Sam Wang called these details "source memory." This kind of memory apparently consists of both the learned content and the specifics of its origin.

Over time, in the process of repeatedly recalling and applying the learned content, our brains eventually transfer the learned content to a different brain structure for efficient storage. In that process, the specifics of its origin are dropped. Aamodt and Wang extended this explanation of source memory to include content information we recall and communicate to other persons. The authors further explained that this content information could include such things as a rumor we heard but didn't verify as truthful. They also say that we typically disregard or fail to accept information that conflicts with our worldview. This seems to suggest that we may disregard or disavow what others tell us, false or not, if it disagrees with what we already believe.

Emotion: Our Hidden Minefield

You likely feel that you know everything about emotion, and you probably do. Nearly every adult likely has experienced just about every kind of emotion that exists. The list is endless. Obviously, this discussion refers to our conscious emotions. Emotion-laden unconscious behavioral responses come from implicit memory. Typically, these are beyond conscious reach.

The quality of any conscious emotion seems able to affect different people differently. What we normally call emotion is the sensation we feel in response to a person, an event, or an experience. Because emotion may exist in a variety of feelings, the plural "emotions" is used too. Most often, an emotion seems to have a particularly impressionable effect on us. Whether positive or negative, it may preempt conscious reasoning. As a result, we often act before we think. Perhaps the best examples of this are the survival and procreative instincts. Road rage is another. Acting on emotion alone poses potential risks. So it seems reasonable that these risks are amplified when emotion is *unconsciously and unintentionally* associated with implicit memories. As such, they seem to represent a minefield of devastating potential.

As mentioned earlier, two capabilities seem to separate humans from most other animals: self-consciousness and emotion. Some people seemed convinced that animals occasionally can express emotion. But self-consciousness apparently never has been demonstrated in animals. Animals have demonstrated what seem to be implicit learned responses. It seems inconclusive, however, how far this extends beyond their traditional instincts of survival and procreation. In his book *Consciousness, Emotional Self-Regulation, and the Brain*, Mario Bureauregard established that different neural processes exist for implicit and explicit emotional processes. The implicit process seems to have pre-existed the explicit on the evolutionary timetable, as possibly essential for survival.

One of the past quarter-century's leading thinkers about emotions, Robert C. Solomon (2003, 2006), has grappled with emotion, trying to make sense of it and to understand its ramifications. The spectrum of emotion seems limitless, its meaning may differ among us, and yet it seems as real as life itself. Earlier, my book implicated the amygdalae of our brains in moderating fear responses, both emotional and physiological. It remains to be explored whether they are similarly involved with other emotions.

Science of Emotion

There are many theories about how our emotions are affected by our perceptions—how we feel about what we see. Now the reverse may be true—can we effect a change in our emotions by altering what we *think* about what we see? Of course, this means considering emotion to be like a spectrum of colors with a range from something like fear to assurance, from sadness to joy, from anxiety to perfect calm, and so forth. A personally felt threat to safety invokes the residual function of the reptilian brain to fight or flight, without intermediate reasoning.

But for other negative feelings or emotion, such as anxiety, depression, sadness, anger, or hate, do humans have any control?

One way we can consider improving negative emotion is provided in our brains. Nature routes most perceptions through our cognitive or reasoning centers. Tied in with such processing are influences like our beliefs, attitudes, and moods. But implicit responses bypass this reasoning. Therefore, evaluating some situations that evoke negative reactions may seem beyond reach. Still, there may be moments of insight that help us reevaluate and come to terms with these.

In our explicit consciousness, we have an innate potential called empathy. It's not always easy to exhibit empathy and many of us would prefer not to even try. Imagine yourself in the following situation. A good friend approaches you and lambastes you mercilessly. Strange, you think, he's never acted this way before. Incidentally, you're having a rotten day: you just had your faithful pet of fifteen years put down due to illness, your spouse and kids are depressed, and you just failed to close a big deal. Your consternation about your friend's behavior likely succumbs to what seems like an affront from your friend, a threat to your self-esteem. No one would criticize you for retaliating equally strongly; after all, isn't that human nature? Giving your friend the benefit of the doubt is not. But maybe, just like you, your friend is having the most miserable day of his life. So he takes it out on you. Maybe, just maybe, in the depths of his friendship, he hopes you'll be understanding and see beyond his ornery façade.

We also have an innate potential called self-reflection, which involves nobody but the individual. For some reason, our emotion seems to feed upon itself. This is especially true with guilt and rumination. Barring psychopathology, we should be able to some extent to control the direction of the spiral, up or down. But, again, this doesn't seem to be human nature. I may be among the worst offenders. I take anti-depressant and anti-panic attack medicines. Still, I never seem to remain in a stable, confident, optimistic mood for very long. Some would say that this comes from the stress of 24/7 caring for my wife and concomitant concerns for our family members in today's precarious world. I can be pretty good at being empathetic toward others. But I find that correcting my negative mood swings usually depends on getting myself "outside my head." In effect, this means my switching from an ineffectual to an effectual spectator. I must focus on taking care of the here and now instead of letting my mind dwell on my shortcomings, failures, or imagined guilt.

Another way the information overload can potentially devastate interpersonal relations depends on our ability to "shift gears." We seem more able to control this in a conscious emotional state than with programmed behavioral responses. For example, perhaps we are absorbed in an important project or trying to get the kids ready for school or otherwise mentally engaged in "busywork." An abrupt interruption—a phone call, a neighbor dropping by, or a boss wanting something—might sorely tax our emotional impulsivity.

Impulsivity and Compulsivity

Impulsivity can be either behavioral or cognitive. The former is more of a failure to think before acting, and the latter seems an inability to act with judgment. But, for the purposes of this book, behavioral impulsivity often is linked to implicit memory in producing an unconscious, unintentional reaction to a particular stimulus. Impulsivity sometimes may be related to self-control, if the person is aware of his or her reaction, as in road rage. But even though the person may be conscious of his or her behavior, he or she may be unable conscientiously to justify or control it.

Compulsivity appears to be a behavioral trait, as in obsessive-compulsive disorder, in which the person may be well aware what he or she is doing but is unable to stop it. As you'll read later in regard to his new treatment of OCD, Jeffrey Schwartz called the conscious awareness an "ineffectual spectator." Oldham, Hollander, and Skodol challenge the idea that impulsivity is different from compulsivity, so far as underlying causes are involved.

Gut Reactions: Yes, They Exist!

People sometimes use the term "gut reaction" to describe the basis of their personal judgment about an idea or their response to certain situations. This actually has its basis in biological fact. Gut reaction has been defined as a judgment that a person quickly becomes aware of, but without knowing its source. It is not a reasoned reaction to an obvious stimulus, but it conveys urgency similar to a thoughtful conviction. Intuition is said to be a good example. Fear may trigger a gut reaction. Perceived danger instinctively can shift our physiology to a fight or flight mode. "The Brain From Top to Bottom: The Amygdala and Its Allies," mentioned earlier, helps explain the mechanism. In such situations, the term "gut reaction" seems appropriate as your muscles tighten, your blood pressure rises, and your stomach is said to "get tied up in knots." There remains a question as to whether a conditioned response in our implicit memory also can induce a gut reaction. It seems reasonable to assume so.

There also is something called "somatic" memory. This typically occurs in abuse. The results need not be evident in physical marks but they can leave "somatic" or bodily impressions. These later may manifest themselves in all manner of bodily, hence "somatic," complaints. Physicians may be at a loss to explain the symptoms or to treat the patient. The patient eventually may become reluctant to seek care for fear of being regarded as a hypochondriac.

Stop the Clamor

You have the power to stop arguments, but you won't like the remedy. It's unnatural, self-defeating, sometimes humiliating, and always unilateral. But it's so obvious and obnoxious that it's usually disregarded. Simply shut up! Leave it be! I had a personal experience of being humiliated in front of many of my friends. I was criticized for forwarding political e-mails that I had not validated. My doing so was inexcusable, to be sure. But rather than perpetuate the disagreement in an attempt to excuse or defend myself, I chose to simply drop the matter.

People consider the human brain a marvelous entity. But few of us realize its infinite complexity and the natural precision that has characterized its evolution over time. Furthermore, the growth and development of the brain in each new human being follows a similar natural plan. This makes it susceptible to many influences at each stage. The next chapter studies this amazing creation from the beginning.

CHAPTER NINE

FROM THE BEGINNING

What Role Did Evolution Play?

THE ANCESTRAL INFLUENCE ON OUR minds and on our behavior stretches back into the eons of time, as humankind adapted to its changing environmental and cultural influences. It's not an easy path to track, and I suspect that some people will disavow its existence. Therefore, the following evolutionary information has been distilled from Joseph Chilton Pearce's (2002) seminal book *The Biology of Transcendence: A Blueprint of the Human Spirit.* This includes his citations of discoveries by other highly creditable researchers too across the globe and over time. But why has this any importance to us today? As you will see, it laid the foundations over time for how our bodies operate today. Also, it emphasizes how much control we do and don't have over our behavior and the implications of this in today's society. Imagine the earliest ancestors of humankind on earth. If evolution is a fact, the following seems reasonable, given the millennia of time available for it to happen.

Pearce described four stages of development of the human brain: first the "inherited" reptilian brain; second, the old mammalian brain; third, the new mammalian brain or neocortex; and fourth, the prefrontal lobes. Each was an addition, not a replacement. He also discussed a fifth separate brain—surprisingly, the heart brain! The heart brain is least recognized as such. Yet it is vitally interdependent with our cranial brain. I will discuss this later.

It is worth noting that each evolutionary step built upon, enhanced, and expanded the potential of the existing system. In other words, nature never seems to abandon that which works. It just continues to try to improve. Each individual stage existed and served well the needs of its hosts for inconceivably long periods of time until it was joined by the next. Each had specific functions and, for the most part, those functions still exist in us today! An example is the sense-and-response system of the reptilian brain. Nature plans for growth and development in a stepwise fashion. It never occurs helter-skelter. Nature has an inherent flexibility to facilitate that growth and development. Apparently, one of the primary mediators is the intelligence of living cells. Evolutionary time seems inconceivably long to those of us for whom minutes sometimes seem like an eternity. Nothing changed overnight. Unfortunately, the indeterminate time frames in which gradual improvements did occur apparently left few paleontological records by which to chart them.

Contrast the intent and impact of each of the first four stages of brain development. The first was the reptilian brain, exemplified in the crocodile and alligator. This was a quick sense-and-respond system, producing action without thought. Learned behavior was performed beneath awareness. Similarly, many decisions were made unconsciously and performed unintentionally to ensure natural functions of the body. The next, the old mammalian brain, gave the owner a new sense of self and the world. It also was called the limbic or emotional-cognitive brain. This new addition gave humans a tool to evaluate their environment and their relationships.

Further along came the new mammalian brain, also called the neo-cortex or verbal-intellectual. This advance enabled the human to stand outside the existing scene, evaluate it, and react accordingly. This was a far cry from the reptilian response mechanism that still colors our implicit and procedural imprinted behavior. Pearce labeled these three advances roughly as three stages, according to added ability: action, feeling, and thinking.

According to Pearce and other researchers, nature's newest addition was the prefrontal cortex (or lobes), which apparently debuts after birth. By contrast, the reptilian antecedent starts functioning in the first trimester of gestation, the old mammalian or limbic in the second, and the new mammalian or neocortex in the third. It literally is impossible to conceptualize the millions of years required for the brain to evolve this far. Nature continually builds upon itself. It discards the inefficient and unproductive and enhances that which is worthwhile.

The Fetal and Newborn Brain

To build a credible case for implicit memory, it seems worthwhile to examine the stages of development of the neuroanatomy of a baby. This helps us recognize the magnitude of changes over time and the implications of each. There always seems to be disagreement about when life begins in the womb. Scientists now claim that the fetus has a primitive brain within a month or so after conception, and by nine months it has virtually all the nerve cells, called neurons, it ever is likely to have. An essential part of the brain's development is the formation of connections, called synapses, between these neurons. It is claimed that, during the first three years of life, the brain creates trillions of new connections. This involves complex circuitry that facilitates the infant's growth and development. Enough of this occurs before birth to provide the fetus with such neuromotor capabilities as movement in the womb. Apparently, too, there is development of certain parts of the brain, such as the amygdalae, as well as the neural pathways that involve the sensory nervous system. These have been shown to be involved in the fetus's registering implicit memory.

Interestingly, the brain seems to overproduce the quantity of connections. It then "prunes" the surplus over time. Perhaps it's the vast quantity of neurons available plus the immense variety of connections required. Somehow, those junctions that experience repeated use are strengthened and those that don't are eliminated or put to alternative use. The average human brain has about one hundred billion neurons, and about a thousand times that many synapses or connections. But even a child might ask how a minute amount of tissue—a brain cell— can process, communicate, and store vast quantities of information. Researchers know that each cell has multiple "arms" branching out and each branch has multiple hairlike growths sprouting out. Also, each cell "communicates" with others using physicochemical spurts between them. In his article "Brain Cells, Doing Their Job with Some Neighborly Help" in the December 25, 2007, *New York Times*, Benedict Carey reported some fascinating findings. Using very specialized techniques, scientists found that when a cell sends out a message, the recipient is not just another single cell. Instead, receptors on neighboring cells also volunteer. Imagine the combined power available.

Both before and after a child's birth, the environment heavily influences the formation of these connections. Apparently, they can flower or fail depending on what the child experiences. Marian Diamond and Janet Hopson's book *Magic Trees of the Mind* provides remarkable insights. The complex relationship between the brain and the environment that begins in the womb continues throughout adolescence. The book's title seems derived from the fact that the environment can significantly affect the development of neuron branches in the brain. Research has shown that three-month-old fetuses have begun listening to their mothers. They seem to have an uncanny ability to recognize her voice. Researchers now are amazed how fetuses develop "deeply embedded" beliefs: about themselves, others, the world at large, and particularly interpersonal relationships.

Newborns actually may be able to begin understanding other languages through their first year. Sucking on a pacifier seems a way to pass time. But research shows that they stop when their interest is attracted by something. Newborns also seem able to recognize stories or music they heard as fetuses. Peter Hepper (1996, 2008), of Queen's University, Belfast, Ireland, even has experimented with the possible impact of environmental sounds. He examined the potentially beneficial effects of stimulating the fetal brain by playing recorded music.

Those who read my previous book *Love and Immortality* may remember that at least one researcher claims that an immortal soul joins the fetus in the early months of gestation. The soul melds its energy with that of the fetus. It also offers comfort and support to the fetus to help prepare it for the shock of childbirth.

The Moderator Brain

In stark contrast to the development of the first three parts of the brain, the fourth—the prefrontal cortex (or lobes)—is a real latecomer. Researchers say that its early development begins after birth and continues until around age fifteen, the time of mid-adolescence. Then, this part of the brain begins a substantial growth spurt, which is not completed until about age twenty-one. Much of the prefrontal cortex's development therefore occurs during a particularly crucial time—puberty. It's a time when the teenager is subjected to a barrage of internal and external influences. These range from hormone surges and a desire for independence to peer competition and rifts with the family. This creates a period ripe for mental problems, from anxiety and depression to frank psychopathology.

As mentioned earlier, the newborn's brain will have acquired the majority of its neurons very early. Yet, the continuing process of wiring and rewiring of connections is not substantially complete until young adulthood. This means that the brain's growth and development, with the help of nature's planning, will experience two periods of intense susceptibility to its environment and its life experiences. The first extends from childhood to mid-adolescence. The second continues to age twenty-one or so.

The prefrontal cortex, therefore, serves a vital coordinating role as it develops in parallel with later developments in the other three parts of the brain. In a sense, it facilitates a more integrated functioning of the other three parts. This is to create a more "civilized" status for the whole. It eventually serves a coordinating function for all of the brain.

If nurturing and care have implemented nature's plan, the prefrontal cortex exhibits a remarkable development between its forward portions and the highest portion of the old mammalian (emotional-cognitive) brain. This begins at the end of the first year, during which the prefrontal cortex started developing, and this development is greatest during the second year of life. This connection is called the orbitofrontal loop. It is responsible for the neural connections upon which an individual's relationships and mental capacities in life depend. Pearce stressed that its importance is "impossible to overestimate." Fulfillment of its function depends on the care toddlers receive and their emotional state as they step forward to explore their world. Researcher Allan Shore provided more information on the importance of this development in his paper "The Experience-Dependent Maturation of a Regulatory System in the Orbital Prefrontal Cortex and the Origin of Developmental Psychopathology" in *Development and Psychopathology*.

Development and growth of the orbitofrontal loop seems to be in keeping with nature's unfolding plan for human growth and development. There are several steps for the growth spurt of the orbitofrontal loop between the ages of fifteen and twenty. According to Pearce (2002), these include several identifiable stages. First, a "poignant and passionate idealism" develops in early puberty. This is followed by a conscious expectation in the mid-teens of some sort of transcendence. Later, there appears an unparalleled belief in what he or she might accomplish. But these further stages may never occur. This malfunction has been attributed largely to society's interference with nature's plan for motherly nurturing, intimacy, and interpersonal communication with the infant.

Critical Periods

Researchers generally agree that babies go through certain critical periods of development early in life. Part of this seems to relate to the distinction between implicit and explicit memory. Apparently, we may unconsciously experience events and emotions that can shape the neuronal wiring which govern our later abilities. Once formed, this "wiring" may be difficult to change.

For example, some children may have a less than complete emotional development. This includes those who undergo severe disruptions before their development of cognition and explicit memory, such as the loss of a mother. One significant role of the mother is to teach her child emotions and attachment. This involves using non-verbal interactions, the music of her voice, and reassuring gestures and touches. That crucial period lasts from around ten to twelve months to sixteen to eighteen months of age. It seems that a key area of the right frontal lobe develops during this time to ensure consistency of human attachments and to regulate emotions. Freud argued that human sexuality and the ability to love depend on what he called "phases of organization" in early childhood. This can affect our capacity to love and to relate to others later in life.

Some researchers feel that critical periods are not so limiting in child development. They believe that nature demonstrates compensatory mechanisms in many children. But it is generally agreed that brain systems depend on environmental stimuli to grow and develop, and that different systems "had rapid, formative growth" during certain periods. Norman Doidge discussed this in his book *The Brain That Changes Itself: Stories of Personal Triumph from the Frontiers of Brain Science.*

The Teenage Brain

As mentioned in the previous section, the moderator part of the brain develops over a very long period of time. It tries to coordinate functions of the three earlier-developed brains. It also seeks to present to the world a maturing human being. The three earlier brains each have inherent functions established over time. By contrast, the fourth brain seems to start from scratch, as it were. Its goal is to accommodate influences from the other three brains as well as influences from the brain's environment (as defined earlier).

The moderator's growth period stretches some twenty years. Thus, this would seem to make it subject to an almost incomprehensible and inexhaustible multitude of environmental demands. No two individuals are exposed to an identical set of environmental influences over this period. There may be generically similar circumstances such as peer pressure. But the nature of this influence and of the individual's response to it can vary substantially. It may be appropriate to wonder what kind of personality becomes a submissive follower and what sort becomes an independent thinker.

Researchers claim that adolescents are more prudent today than even five years ago. Yet, as mentioned earlier, research suggests that teenagers require an excessively high level of stimulus, even brutal thrills, to satisfy their self-perceived needs. Risky behaviors abound. Some young people self-induce unconsciousness. Others partake of a random mix of parents' prescription drugs sneaked away to a party. Yet no amount of wisdom offered by older persons, especially parents, is tolerated for fear of humiliation by peers. Only those accounts of fatalities that reach the news media cause the rest of us to pause briefly. But there continue to be soon-forgotten moments of sympathy and firm parental assurances of "never my child."

"Heartfelt," we say, meaning sincere. But would you ever believe that our hearts are also brains? Check out the next chapter to learn why.

CHAPTER TEN

THE HEART OF IT ALL

The Heart Brain

THERE IS WHAT PEARCE (2002) and other leading researchers designate as a "fifth brain." It is located within the heart and linked with the brain in our head. This may seem impossible, yet researchers around the country have substantiated it. The human heart long has been considered the seat of feelings. It apparently has an emotional force sufficient to influence intentions and behavior. This is not just whimsical or poetic; it has a firm basis in scientific fact.

The following scientific revelations about the heart brain were shocking to me, even as a pharmacist. They are listed below individually to allow you to consider each one's special significance.

- The heart is the center of an electromagnetic field that extends as far as fifteen feet from the body.
- An electrocardiograph does not need to be connected to the body—readings can be made with electrodes as far as three feet from the heart.
- Each heartbeat generates two and one-half watts of electrical energy—enough to light a small electric bulb.
- A single isolated heart cell will continue to beat but only for a short while—it eventually gets out of sync and dies.
- Two heart cells, even separated by a small distance, resonate and remain alive.

- Heart and brain frequencies become synchronous in experimental procedures wherein stress is reduced.
- As many as 60 to 65 percent of heart cells are neurons, like brain cells.
- The same neurotransmitters that function in the brain also function in heart ganglia.
- Certain neural ganglia in the heart have direct connections with the emotional-cognitive centers of the brain.
- A continuing dialogue exists between the heart and the brain, in sensing and alerting one another and in directing actions of the body to preserve well-being.

About 80 percent of brain mass is composed of what are called "glial cells." They are named after the Latin word for glue. These are electromagnetically sensitive. They are claimed to form electromagnetic fields in the brain separate and distinct from the electrochemical fields involving neurons. Little else is known about them.

Another level of heart-brain influence seems hormonal. Pearce (2002) cited a *Scientific American* cover story that announced the finding by a group of French physicians, Roget et al., that the atrium area of the heart produces a hormone labeled ANF, which can mediate the functions of the emotional-cognitive system.

Human Energy Fields

Valerie Hunt conclusively demonstrated the existence of subtle energy forces, or fields, operating in and around the human body. She was able to demonstrate the existence of what are labeled "chakras" and "auras," to show variation in both magnitude and frequency of such energy, and to document correlations of electromagnetic measurements at chakras with aura observations. Her studies suggested that detectable changes in these energy fields might help reveal health disorders.

Hunt also reported a surprising finding. Some stimuli elicit a response in the energy field, as registered in the aura, before they do in the brain, as measured by brain waves. These include an inadvertent sound, light flashes, and even a feather touching the aura but not the skin. This delay in brain response apparently also was observed when a change in one person's energy field vibration affected another person's field. In some inexplicable way, the mind seemed to interact with these electromagnetic energy fields.

National Institutes of Health researchers Pert and Snyder studied the activity of neuropeptides. They had previously believed that brain neurochemicals and their receptors worked like locks and keys. Then, they discovered that when brain neuropeptides were stimulated, cell neuropeptides in remote areas of the body were activated immediately. This was too fast to have been caused by chemical or nerve transmission signals. Pert and Snyder now feel that the brain functions as part of a vibratory energy field. They discussed this in their report "Opiate Receptor: Demonstration in Nervous Tissue."

Pearce (2002) differentiated three well-known means by which some electrical activity in the body is measured. One is electrical energy created by brain nerve cells, recorded by an electroencephalogram (EEG). A second is electrical energy generated by muscles and measured by an electromyogram (EMG). A third is electrical heart activity picked up by an electrocardiogram (EKG). The three signals can differ from one another in frequency patterns and strengths.

Remember the science-fiction devices used by Flash Gordon and Dick Tracy? Well, two innovative ones now have been developed to utilize the science of bioenergetics. One is called a superconducting quantum interference device (SQUID). This is a highly sensitive magnetometer that is said to map biomagnetic fields in the body. A former Ford Motor Company scientist spearheaded its development. Another is a computerized instrument based on "gas discharge visualization." It utilizes Kirlian photography and is claimed to allow real-time observation of human energy fields. The latter device was developed at the St. Petersburg (Russia) State Technical University. These instruments are discussed in "Some Key Reiki Concepts."

Morphic Form and Fields

Related to the fact of human energy fields is the concept of morphic form and morphic fields. These refer to some researchers' belief that the "form" of each biological entity, from the smallest cell to the entire human body, is a product of a "morphic" energy field. That is, this field is responsible for the characteristic nature of the entity. This makes us what we are almost from the moment of conception.

Our characteristic of morphic forms is that they are not cast in stone. If this is true, it might be a reason for miraculous healings. As an example, Melvin Morse told of an eight-year-old boy with a very rare genetic defect that universally was considered fatal by the teenage years. One day, when the boy neared death, all the cells in his body suddenly became normal. Something had repaired his genetic code.

This acknowledges that each part of the human body has properties that do not explain how all of them work together synergistically. It appears that the complexity of our bodies cannot fully be explained in mechanistic or physicochemical terms. Like electromagnetic and gravitational fields, morphic fields cannot physically be seen, but can be demonstrated by their detectable effect. It also appears that such fields can influence, or resonate with, one another *even at a distance.* Remember that one heart cell alone will die, but two placed side by side can resonate in sync.

The following experiment will seem absurd, but it actually has produced an outcome that further adds to this dilemma. A group (A) of rats in one laboratory was taught certain new behaviors. In a remote laboratory, two different groups (B and C) of rats also were taught those behaviors. The speed with which groups B and C each learned those behaviors was measured and compared. Group B was timed *before* group A learned them and group C *after* group A did. It was demonstrated that rats in group C learned faster than group B did; in other words *after* group A had learned them!

Now stop a minute. Think back to your earliest recollection. Imagine you are that child again. Maybe even lie on the floor and look up. You'll get the most out of the next chapter from that perspective— like a newcomer fresh out of the womb.

CHAPTER ELEVEN

WELCOME TO THE WORLD

NEARLY EVERYONE HAS EXPERIENCED BEING a newcomer: in a new community, new school, new church, new job, or even a new family. Imagine the last time you were a newcomer. How old were you? How much support did you have from your family or others? Was this the first time for you? These and many other conditions helped determine how comfortable you were in adapting to the required changes. You may have had some experience watching others adjust to new circumstances, and this may have reinforced your ability to deal with your situation.

The World As Sensed by the Newcomer

But just think what it must be like as a new baby, living inside your mother's womb for nine months. Then, you suddenly are projected into a bright, noisy, and confusing place. By contrast, if you move as a teenager or an adult, you may have advance notification and maybe even a chance to learn something about your new place ahead of time.

Recent scientific publications assert that we have totally misjudged new babies, grossly underestimating their capabilities even as fetuses. Numerous researchers now characterize babies as enthusiastic learners about their new world. New parents may excitedly await their child's first words and first steps. However, we don't realize that babies come fully equipped to experience most of an adult's emotions by the time they are born. You read earlier that the fetus can sense whether it is expected, wanted, and positively anticipated. Imagine the newborn's eagerness to confirm visually its earlier beliefs or suspicions.

For a fetus or infant, the word *experience* is a key term. Most of us would question the reality of implicit memory before or soon after birth. Our days are filled with words that have meaning to us. But babies don't start learning, understanding, and using words for a couple of years. So how could they *comprehend* anything? But imagine yourself at a funeral or a celebration in a foreign language. Close your eyes. Can you easily distinguish between the two? The words have no meaning, but you have a distinct *sense* of what's happening. Perhaps intuition is a better example, since the feeling may seem not only extraordinary but also characteristically silent. It cannot be denied, although many of us ignore intuition.

Faces and voices crowd the newcomer's arrival. His or her vision or hearing may be imperfect at first, but those senses include enough recognition characteristics to know who's who. Also, his or her implicit memory system is quite adequate to store vital information about the environment. Since it is obvious that science has no means of directly assessing specific fetal beliefs, researchers say we must "listen to the language" of prenates and newborns. This involves carefully monitoring variations in posture, movements, facial expressions, attention, gestures, and even breathing and heart rates.

In his report "Prenatal Memory and Learning" on the Life Before Birth Web site, David Chamberlain points to newborns' "language" capability, first exhibited by voluntary movements about ten weeks into gestation and continuing to develop in the womb. Their senses include at least "touch, thermal experiences, taste, odor, hearing, licking, sucking, and even vision." Newborns have a wide range of communicating with the mother and others both verbally and nonverbally. The latter include "body color, emotional behaviors, withdrawal, hand gestures, a range of facial statements, instant imitation, and lip-reading." CBS's *The Early Show* included a feature "What Newborns Are Really Thinking," which provided a sneak preview of a newcomer's look at the world. "They are doing much more than sleeping, eating, and crying."

The newcomer is especially sensitive to interpersonal relationships. These involve not just those shared with his or her mother while in the womb or as a "helpless" newborn. A baby also senses relationships *between* his or her parents and with other caregivers. As an example, babies know whether or not they are wanted.

Trust seems to be perhaps the basic attribute that newcomers offer parents and significant others. It also is what each of us searches for in one another. Loss of trust may be more devastating for fetuses and babies, since the rest of us usually have become accustomed to the bumps and grinds of life. Some of us have had such negative experiences with other people, in both our implicit and explicit memories, that distrust is an automatic response when we meet a new person. Social experiences of the newborn soon alert them to whether their world is a friendly place. "Social" means both interacting with family, caregivers, and others and *watching* them carefully and unobtrusively. Some people say that fetuses, newborns, and young children are like sponges, absorbing everything around them. Ever hear a two-year-old utter a cuss word without any idea what it means?

A Newcomer's Vigilance

The newborn's apparently humble status disguises the intricate memory and evaluation system that has been at work from early in the womb. Memory means the implicit memory and evaluation means the emotional component of each implicit memory. Both are subconsciously registered. But they may be primed or stimulated by circumstances much later in life to elicit a particular internal bodily or external behavioral response.

The newborn's brain is said to be especially sensitive to voices, faces, and information about others provided by social interaction. Multiple, repeated experiences of social interaction apparently register and shape something called "implicit relational knowing." Nature provides for infants to become accustomed to the voices of birth parents, especially during the intimate fetal time with the mother. Imagine a newborn's confusion when he or she is thrown into a new environment characterized by radically different vocal characteristics. Adoptive parents should be aware of this.

Infants even are said to have a sort of intuition. This helps them "read" other people's intentions and resonate empathetically in reassuring situations. Neurobiologists claim that this is a form of implicit memory that guides infants' behaviors with intimate others as well as their flow of emotions. The infant brain therefore seems dependent on social experiences to assess whether his or her new environment is basically friendly or threatening.

Consider that few young children watch television alone. Even when the mother uses it as a distraction to keep her child entertained, she or others wander into the room from time to time. So the child sees not only the television screen, but also watches Mom's and others' reactions. Even a silent smile or frown by them about what's being televised may register with the child. Actually, the mother's or others' reactions to what is happening on TV may be more useful to the young child, as he or she continually searches for cues about his or her new world. The same potential holds for the impressionable young child observing other people's behavior, particularly parents and siblings. Remember, the young child considers the attitudes, beliefs, and behavior of authority figures to be the "gospel truth," never to be questioned. It must be wondered how soon older siblings' behavior influence a young child's view of the world, even in advance of later peer pressures.

Also related to neonatal development is a condition known as "object constancy." This has been defined as the perception by a very young baby that the object of its attention—such as its mother—retains its identity with all its attributes despite separation, altered appearance, or change of setting. In a sense, this provides the infant's "security blanket." As the child matures, object constancy assumes a different role. It helps shape the youngster's ability to separate perceptually as a "self," a secure identity or personality of its own. The term that psychologists use for the latter is "identity formation." Psychoanalyst Margaret Mahler coined the term "internal mother" in 1975 for the initial stage of object constancy. It is discussed in detail in the book *The Internal Mother: Conceptual and Technical Aspects of Object Constancy,* edited by Salman Akhtar and colleagues.

There are numerous studies documenting infants' voice-recognition skills ensuring the close presence and protection of the mother. This seems reminiscent of the same skills that offspring of wild animals have. This might well contribute to the mother-child bond. It also may reinforce the idea that nurture can play as important a role as nature with regard to parent-child bonding. Associated with recognition skills and bonding is another kind of "imprinting," different from implicit memory imprinting. This other kind is a remarkable event said to occur within the first few hours of birth. It seems most evident in animals, when a newborn for some reason is exposed to an animal that is not its natural parent—or even to a human being. This exposure "imprints" or bonds the newborn with the creature to which it is exposed. Readers undoubtedly have heard or seen examples of a duck living with chickens, not aware it is different. Wildlife experts who rescue orphaned newborn animals encounter such a problem. If human caregivers are allowed to imprint on these babies, the mature animals have great difficulty being returned to the wild.

Meanwhile, it seems reasonable to expect that the infant's implicit memory system would be operating full time. The baby might form either reassuring or negative impressions about its care. Impossible, some persons still would insist. Some people apparently still hold the view that nothing significant happens until a child can walk, talk, understand, and reason.

What Sort of Welcome Awaits?

It has been advocated that parents should begin preparing for the birth of their child as early as conception, or even before conception. Recent advances in pathology now suggest that diseases which affect us as adults can be traced to the entire gestation period. The mother-to-be's endocrine system intimately affects the growth and development of the fetus. Remember that nature has provided for the mother to prepare the newborn for surviving in the environment in which she lives. In doing so, she sends the same "signals" to the fetus's target cells, tissues, and organs that she sends throughout her own body, helping her cope with daily exigencies. It is no wonder that the offspring comes already conditioned to the stresses of the mother's everyday life.

How do you, as a teenager or adult, react to being criticized? Imagine how a newcomer feels. He or she has no ability to question or analyze the condemnation. It comes from an authority figure. Still, he or she may feel hurt, betrayed, and shamed. It registers in his or her implicit memory system with strong emotional overtones. If left uncorrected, and particularly if repeated often, it may become the template through which the toddler views any future criticism, even as an adult. The original criticism may have been justifiable at the time as viewed by the parent or other caregiver. But it is incumbent on the adult to help the child deal with such a negative, probably unexpected, judgment.

Mental health professionals say it is vital to use such situations as learning experiences for the child. It is important for the parent or caregiver to explain, in a loving manner that the youngster can understand, why he or she was criticized and any particular restrictions imposed as a result. It is equally important to reassure the child that he or she is unconditionally loved. Child development researchers say that a young child's repeated storage of images of disapproval, without commensurate reassurances of love, can lead to his or her becoming overly inhibited, defensively hostile, and even clinically depressed.

Shame is inevitable in life. Role modeling by the parent can help the child positively deal with mistakes. This should help provide the youngster a self-confidence that later enables him or her to cope with life's demands and to move forward. Obviously, once the child is older and has developed both a verbal ability and an emerging self-concept, he or she may be less likely to accept a parent's behavior as authoritative. However, we are told that this typically does not start until age three to four.

The term "attachment," or emotional bond, seems to hold a special meaning for babies, perhaps stemming from nine months in the womb. Attachment also seems to have some social significance for the newborn. This may be mediated through his or her newfound experiences of separation, reunion, and accessibility following nine months in total attachment to the mother. It also can affect relationships with significant others. Brain research shows that attachment is actually a regulatory system that develops during infancy and early childhood. Early trauma usually reduces a child's ability to self-regulate feelings of affection, despite the best efforts of adoptive parents.

Anne Gearity has studied adopted children with attachment disorder. She contrasts adopted children who have spent time with caregivers other than parents with adopted children who have not. Attachment disorder is more likely in the latter group. Imprints of irretrievable loss—implicit memories so emphatic that nothing consistently seems to remedy them—are typical. She reported her findings in her presentation "Reactive Attachment Disorder: Mining Gold Using a Child's Map of Attachment" on the Minnesota Adoption Support and Preservation Web site.

Gearity warns adoptive parents that, as the old saying goes, "time heals all wounds." There is no instant magic. It is as though the child's perception of the adoptive parents' reliability and trustworthiness may vary from day to day. Adopted children, in turn, may fail to respond in ways the adoptive parents hoped for or expected. Such parents must realize that it's nothing personal. Gearity says it takes "extraordinary patience" to get in sync with the adopted child's perception of the world. After all, the child's anticipation of welcoming, caring natural parents has been shattered.

The disruption of newcomers' lives is securely imprinted in their implicit minds. Although they are not consciously reminded by it, there is a primitive natural expectation that is unfulfilled. Certain ages are especially critical: five to six, when they may realize they are adopted; adolescence, when they are trying to express their independence; and older teenage years, when they conceptually become independent.

The Bond of Nurture

To young parents, their first baby can be a very maturing experience, but sometimes it becomes disruptive for them. What used to be a twosome is now a threesome. Despite the awe and love that we hope both mother and father feel for their new family member, the parents' freedom and responsibility have changed dramatically. There seems to be a different kind of attraction the baby has for each of the parents. Nature established a natural bond between the mother and baby. But a controversy still seems to exist over whether nature or nurture is most responsible for the bonding. The term "attachment" almost seems synonymous with bond.

"Attunement" is another term that is recognized for its significant contribution to bonding and child development. This has been defined as "active participation in exchanges." Marlowe Embree explained the nuances of this relationship on two Web sites. One of the key elements of a secure parent-child bonding seems to be an affectionate eye contact. Apparently, this act has a profound biological effect on the infant. It might be likened to the surge of feel-good brain chemicals—endorphins—that marathon runners and others report. Parental nurturing shapes the offspring's emotional nature from its earliest moments of life. The most welcoming experience for a newborn is the mother's genuine and sustained look of love. This naturally is his or her first visible eye contact with the mother, and it supplements sensations the fetus felt before birth.

Also, it is claimed that such experiences are particularly conducive to maturation of parts of the brain involved in healthy regulation of emotion later in life. In my previous book, I differentiated between actual and mechanical expressions of love, compassion, and similar affections. Similarly, I believe attunement results from an actual rather than a mechanical experience an infant has with another person. This seems to suggest the possibility of emotional resonance, especially with the mother or father.

In their book *Magical Parent-Magical Child, the Optimum Learning Relationship,* Michael Mendizza and Joseph Chilton Pearce recommend a parent-child relationship that some people seem to feel is overly ambitious. But it certainly seems to incorporate the epitome of desirable parenting. Pearce is an eminent child development researcher. Mendizza founded *Touch the Future,* a nonprofit center designed to strengthen learning relationships between adults and children. Their book involves a bilateral process, shared between parent and child. In a sense, their book seeks to rekindle parents' own childhood experiences of discovery, wonder, and learning. They feel that this enables a transformation of the adult and leads to playful, dynamic, and reciprocal relationships that foster the growth and development of the child. The book likens this relationship to those employed by successful coaches in sports and other fields.

This goal becomes particularly pertinent in today's world. Young children may spend most of their time with caregivers rather than parents. The child's life also may be disrupted by such events as abandonment, adoption, divorce, a dysfunctional home, or abuse. All too often, one or both parents may be substance abusers. Such a father may create an atmosphere implying disregard for either the mother or the child or both. Because the mother and the fetus are intimately connected, even such things as mother's state of mind can influence the health of both of them as well as their bonding. Obviously, proper prenatal care is vital, including not just nutrients and conduct. Also, it is important to avoid stress-induced changes in endocrine and other neurological chemicals transferred through the placenta.

Perhaps one of the earliest recorded examples of the mother-child bond was revealed in the biblical account of two women claiming the same baby in an appearance before King Solomon. To settle the dispute, the king ordered that the baby be cut in half and one-half given to each woman. "Wait," said one of the women, "give the baby to her." Then Solomon knew that that woman spoke out of her selfless love for the child, and he awarded her the baby.

Mental health professionals say that children and adults with insecure attachment histories seem more vigilant for perceived threats of abandonment, rejection, or lack of approval. This behavior may be manifested, probably unconsciously, by certain postures, behaviors, or mental states: holding back or withdrawing, avoidance, anxiety, hunger for acceptance, aversion to intimacy, or even shame.

Modeling

This is not a person's exemplifying personal qualities that might stimulate others to emulate him or her, so-called role modeling. Instead, this modeling is at the very crux of human growth and development. This is the presence of what might be called "templates"—for the fetus, the newborn, and the developing child to focus on and to depend upon to fulfill the different stages of development. Without such fulfillment, nature's plan may go awry. This book touches on only a very few of the potential disruptions in the modeling process, to be discussed in a later chapter. As examples, the fetus imprints on the mother's voice as a stimulus for development of the infant's language and sensory-motor systems. The mother's face at birth serves as a stimulus for the newborn's awareness and the initial stage of visual development. Environmental stimuli serve as "models" for nature's plan to unfold.

Interestingly, infants come "hardwired" to see only a single object at birth—a human face! That face serves as the template for the development of their visual system, reaching stability in about nine months. Full development requires some twelve years. In sharp contrast, infants deprived of early face stimulus and its accompanying benefits show no signs of awareness or visual consciousness—for as long as ten to twelve weeks after birth. Over time, this face—hopefully the mother's—serves as the image for which vision gradually accommodates to other objects.

Impact on Fathers

Perhaps surprisingly, bodies of new fathers may help prepare them for nurturing their babies, according to new research. The May 7, 2008, edition of *USA TODAY* announced this in an article with the title "New Dads Twice as Likely to Become Depressed, Study Finds." In an insert to the article "A Hormonal 'Maternal Side'," research suggests that the father's testosterone level drops and his estrogen level increases, strengthening the biological quality of the father-child bond. It long has been recognized that hormonal levels change in new mothers.

The article also points out other potential effects of fatherhood. When babies reach about nine months of age, their fathers seem twice as likely as other men their age to exhibit signs of clinical depression. This was attributed to the added stress on the husband. If the pleasurable aspects of new fatherhood don't manifest themselves, the possible depression can have significant adverse effects on the infant. Depressed fathers are said to read to their kids less often, possibly accounting for their two-year-olds' smaller vocabularies.

The article also quoted researchers at Oxford University who found a link between children's defiant, disobedient, and hostile behavior at age seven and their fathers' depression when their children were two months old. Also, after age three, children may blame themselves for their parents' depression.

Findings in the *USA TODAY* article were from presentations at an American Psychiatric Association meeting in Washington, D.C. The reports seemed to underscore a comment made there by psychiatrist Nada Stotland of Rush Medical College in Chicago, "There aren't any secrets from babies." Moreover, the significance of these findings seemed validated by the increasing role of fathers caring for children.

The Value of Touch

In his book *The Biology of Belief*, Bruce Lipton (2005) cites some fascinating results of studies by James W. Prescott, former director of the National Institutes of Health's section on Human Health and Child Development. These compared how different human cultures raise their children. In a society that loved their children and demonstrated this by physically holding, caressing, and carrying their children throughout much of the day, the culture was peaceful. By contrast, those cultures that deprived their infants, children, and adolescents of extensive caring and touch invariably were violent in nature. It seems that children who didn't receive touch had a high risk of "somatosensory disorder." This usually is characterized by an inability to physiologically suppress surging levels of stress hormones, sometimes leading to violence.

The need for touching is often downplayed. Yet, sustained physical contact in a caring, loving manner is said to be one of a newborn's most reliable indicators of a safe environment. All of us "remember" every emotion and physical sensation we experienced as a fetus and as a young child, despite our conscious inability to recall these. This is implicit memory. The process of forgetting now appears to apply only to our explicit memory. There, we mercifully may repress unbearable conscious memories. Also, as you will read elsewhere in this book, Alzheimer's seems to affect only explicit memory.

Other Environmental Factors

Neuroscientists now seem to believe that the intricate relationship between brain development and the environment may offer new approaches or interventions, particularly for children with special needs. Crawling, for example, has been shown to be especially important in facilitating a child's ease of reading.

Scientists feel that babies and young children benefit more from play and interactions with parents and significant others than from such things as flash cards. It seems that enjoyable social experiences provide learning opportunities that encourage an infant's brain to develop. Apparently, children enter this world prepared and eager to discover the environment that awaits them. Here, they find a world where social interaction seems to provide more clues than material objects.

Exploring and discovering their new world also emphasizes the value of young children's social interactions with one another, in both group and everyday settings. This seems to validate parking some young children with a responsible group of caregivers while both parents work, a sort of mixed blessing. For homeschooled children, the need for social encounters might be met by interactions with siblings. The word "parking" was used intentionally. It serves to question several aspects: the nature of care provided; the monitoring of social interaction for positive outcomes; and the extent and nature of complementary care provided by parents at other times. Nature seems to teach parents how to help children learn just as it prepares children to learn.

Mind-Body Connection

A major emphasis in psychotherapy in the past decade or two involves the "mind-body connection." Mind-body principles seem to be effective in working with early disturbance, with severe depression and anxiety, and with trauma and somatic symptoms. Mind-body therapy appears to involve many kinds of "real-life" approaches. These include patterning, role-playing, emotional expression, breath awareness, drawing, movement, meditation, journaling, stretching, and visualization. Susan Aposhyan described this in her book *Mind-Body Psychotherapy: Principles, Techniques, and Practical Applications*. This concept is not radically new: it has its roots in history. Among those who have been intimately involved in mind-body research and therapy are Herbert Benson, Joan Borysenko, Larry Dossey, Bernie Seigal, and Dean Ornish.

Traditional thinking about bearing children still seems focused on appropriate prenatal and nutritional support. Psychological stress and trauma seem inconceivable in a fetus. Research shows that nothing could be further from the truth. We usually view a newborn's symptoms as physically based and treat them accordingly. Only recently have researchers recommended that both physical and emotional needs of a newborn be addressed. A significant number of children in European orphanages died even though they were well fed and received good medical attention. Personal and emotional stimulation was lacking. Adults with similar symptoms might be diagnosed with psychological or psychiatric problems. An early positive attachment is necessary for survival and future physical, mental, and emotional health of our children.

Nurturing somehow also fosters the natural growth and development of the emotional-cognitive system of children. There obviously remains a debate over whether emotional-cognitive changes were more the product of stimulus overload or sensual deterioration precipitated by changed patterns of child rearing. Researchers revealed some startling facts in the past half-century, as mothers moved away from breast-feeding and depended more on caregivers. Pearce (2002) revealed that

American high school students once had a working knowledge of twenty-five thousand words; today, that stands at ten thousand. In 1998, foreign-born students took eighty-five percent of all academic honors in this country.

Rohner and Khaleque presented a parental acceptance-rejection theory (PARTheory) of social development in "Parental Acceptance-Rejection and Life-Span Development: A Universal Perspective," an online reading. It addresses worldwide causes and impacts of parent-infant relationships. Members of every culture and ethnic group studied so far seem consistently to suffer the consequences of perceived parental rejection. This universally appears to be associated with some specific form of psychological maladjustment.

Psychologists also have identified a mother-child relationship called "reciprocal augmentation of responses." Classically, it seems to involve a child's misinterpretation of the parent's reaction to the youngster's behavior. In effect, the child changes his or her behavior to what he thinks is wanted. But if the infant again gets a disapproving look or verbal warning, he or she becomes very confused. This may be exacerbated, especially when the mother is having an internal problem with implicit imprints from her own childhood. An example might be when an infant wants to nurse. The mother wants to be nurturing but she has a buried conflict about breast-feeding from her own mother.

Conceiving, birthing, and rearing offspring is a natural process, ordained by nature. Challenges abound, thereby punctuating joys and sorrows. But life doesn't move in an orderly and predictable fashion. There may be major disruptions. Everyone probably tries to deal with these to the best of his or her ability. But these disruptions can be so demanding, so unanticipated, and so sudden that some of us make bad decisions, actions we may regret later. Let's examine some possibilities.

Chapter Twelve

Disruptions in a Natural Process

Pregnancies may be accompanied by unsettling circumstances. The pregnancy may have been unanticipated or even unwanted. Older couples may "accidentally" conceive; young lovers may disregard the heat of passion; young women may risk compromising situations; and incest or rape may occur. Some babies so conceived are accepted and ostensibly treated as family members. But news reports abound of young, unmarried girls who have disguised their pregnancies and some even have disposed of the babies. Apparently, these girls feared being identified with a hidden pregnancy.

Joint Responsibility

Mothers and fathers share the responsibilities of pregnancy. The father is just as responsible, even though the mother carries the baby. Whatever affects the father also may affect the mother and the fetus! Consider the following: the father's loss of his job, his having an affair with another woman, his abusive treatment of his spouse, his workplace stress, his drug or alcohol abuse, his attitude toward the pregnancy—the list is endless. Despite any effort he makes to hide these or to shield the mother-to-be, she ultimately will sense that something is amiss. Science has shown that the resulting stress she feels can affect the fetus biologically, somatically, and implicitly.

The normal bond between mother and child is thought to begin soon after conception. However, the fetus and the young child can feel threatened by unforeseen and unsettling circumstances of almost any kind. The bond of nurture more nearly can ensure an entirely different outcome, even to the extent of helping develop what mental health professionals call a "resilient child." Resilience is discussed in the next chapter.

Because this book is devoted to the previously unrecognized state of mind of fetuses and very young children, it focuses primarily on the young. But the intent is to help each of us better understand how our behavior—as parents—may have been shaped by our own implicitly conditioned behavioral responses. This may help explain, but not necessarily excuse, how we—as parents—treat each other. Probably more important is how we treat the pregnancy and the newborn.

With regard to health, unwanted children of high-risk teenagers seem to share their mothers' health risks. Such babies are said to be twice as likely to die in their first year as babies born to mothers over twenty years old. Children born to younger girls also seem to show lower achievement scores and problem behaviors in school.

This book also helps to reveal the impact of implicit memory on all of us. You may wonder how fully, when, or if a child becomes consciously aware of his or her abandoned status. A later account adds some dimension to this question through a heart-rending true-life scenario. It is a true experience, described by a family who adopted a Romanian orphan.

This book will not attempt to address all the potential events that can disrupt an otherwise natural process. The major emphasis will be on the mother and the fetus or infant. The emphasis will be on choices or actions by the mother or by both parents that can significantly affect the development, health, and well-being of the fetus or child. Persons who experience these particular disruptions probably never forget them. The outcomes only occasionally receive attention in the news media. Yet it seems worthwhile to examine the intricacies of some of these situations.

Eight such circumstances are considered. The first three—unwanted, abandoned, and abused children—address attitudes and actions by parents. The second two—a dysfunctional home and alcoholic/addicted family—are situational, occurring in an environment not conducive to an offspring's welfare. The sixth—orphanhood or premature death of a parent—is beyond control of parents or child. Similarly, the seventh—divorce—may be beyond parents' control. The eighth—adoption—may present special problems for the adoptive parents. This latter one may not seem to represent a so-called disruption from the adoptive parents' viewpoint. Yet, it very well may be, from the viewpoint of the fetus or child.

Unwanted, Abandoned, and Abused Children

As mentioned earlier, fetuses apparently are able to sense whether or not they are wanted. In addition to the preceding situations, some established families suddenly find that the mother is "accidentally" pregnant. How these families deal with the pregnancy obviously varies. Some do not resort to abortion but attempt to deal with the newcomer as best they can. The family's attitudes and behavior about the circumstances may become obvious to the child, with resulting implications.

Of all the potential disruptions, abandonment may be the most inexcusable. Obviously, it also is fraught with both danger and uncertainty. As mentioned earlier, far too many young, unmarried women have awakened to the stark truth of being pregnant. They immediately are confronted with many issues. These include self-doubts, the risk of shame, the decision of whether or not to seek abortion, not knowing whom to trust, personal despair, covert action, and a variety of other challenges. These can severely affect their personal lives, relationships with parents and peers, scholastic work, and even their personal health. I've been unable to find statistics comparing those pregnant young women who commit suicide with those who elect abortion or destroy the newborn secretly. But all of these possible choices must seem almost overwhelming to these young women. Suddenly, any prior plans for a happy life are crushed.

Abuse of a child is categorically inexcusable. But rape or molestation of a child is even more horrible and introduces a potentially devastating set of circumstances for the youngster. The child's age naturally has a significant influence. He or she previously may have viewed the new world as trustworthy and safe. These acts not only can shatter that perception but also cause a great deal of other visible and invisible lasting damage to him or her.

Before a certain age, apparently around age two to three, children have not yet developed full communicative and reasoning abilities. They have not yet come to grips with what is normal or abnormal in relationships with parents and significant others. Before that, a child actually may accept an adult's deviant behavior without challenge. At some later time, however, the child will recognize what's happening as unnatural. This then forces him or her to confront several choices:

- tell others in hopes they will intervene
- accept that the other parent ignores the event
- believe that the situation is inevitable
- blame himself or herself for causing it
- simply tolerate it

Finding no escape route or accessible help, some children do what psychologists call "dissociate." They intentionally "escape" mentally to avoid the trauma.

To the extent that the act is brutal or the child views the perpetrator or act as life-threatening, stark fear likely will shift all the child's systems into a defensive mode, at least invisibly. The victim's visible behavior likely will differ according to the circumstances. If a person known to the child commits the act—especially after the victim recognizes the act as deviant behavior—the situation and its outcome can escalate. It could produce a lifelong manifold negative impact on the youngster, on the later teenager, and on the eventual adult. The constellation of effects on the child's implicit and explicit memory and on his or her eventual adjustment to life is almost beyond comprehension.

Dysfunctional Home and Alcoholic/Addicted Family

The term "dysfunctional home," like art, often is in the mind of the beholder—in this case, in the mind of a family member. Surveys probably would suggest that many people probably feel that some part of their growing up was dysfunctional.

Any mix of three plus in a family (father, mother, and child) will experience times when one or more members are not satisfied with other members' behavior. Puberty introduces many opportunities for this. Unfortunately, newcomers in multiple sibling families may take offense to how they *perceive* themselves being treated, by parents or siblings. These *implicit* memories—or even *explicit* memories—may last a lifetime. It is important for parents to recognize that they were not the same mother and father to each of their children, no matter how much they try or believe themselves to be. Family circumstances change. Parents change too, as life moves onward. Any of us may harbor imprints from feeling undervalued in a multiple family. So it may be helpful at some point for us personally to come to grips with the reality that each child cannot and will not always be treated equally in his or her perception. Timing and circumstances may be beyond parents' control.

Obviously, alcoholism and addiction induce dysfunctional behavior. The potential negative impact on fetuses and newborns in such surroundings obviously is

limitless. Perhaps the most extreme example is a newborn who is addicted as a result of the mother's addiction. You can imagine, in the context of this book, that there are a variety of possible negative influences on the fetus and on the child, even if the mother is not addicted.

Orphanhood or Premature Death of a Parent

Either of these situations may leave lasting effects upon children, particularly depending upon their age at the time of loss. I will discuss the possible impact later. However, a personal example might help illustrate the potential influence of the death of the father during his wife's pregnancy.

My father died a slow, stressful death from typhoid fever during the month before I was born. My mother must have suffered a literal hell in the process. This was compounded by never-ending criticism from his brothers and sister that my mother was not caring for my father properly. Typhoid is rare in the world today; vaccines are available to prevent it, and antibiotics will treat it. But, in 1932, a patient endured a very high fever and either lived or died. Little could be done to influence the outcome.

Many people likely would disavow any harmful effects on the fetus and newborn in the event of such unsettling influences on the mother. After all, the baby may appear entirely normal. Hardly anyone would expect any kinds of somatic and sensory imprints to be left on the fetus. But science has shown that these can occur. They can leave lasting influences on the growth, well-being, and behavior of the child and even on the subsequent adult.

Divorce

Whatever the reason behind the divorce of parents, both parties likely try to console their children. Siblings' ages and degree of maturity may significantly influence the children's apparent acceptance of the split. Yet, many children still could harbor firm beliefs or misunderstandings that may threaten their self-esteem or welfare. It seems only natural that some offspring of divorcing parents suffer a conviction of personal responsibility. They can suspect that they were, for some undecipherable reason, the cause of the divorce. If this is not detected, and even with efforts to resolve such children's feelings, some damage may occur to them. A slightly different approach to the divorce may occur with children old enough to consciously reason. It may prompt them to undertake an intensive and excruciating self-review of anything they possibly may have done to cause their parents' divorce. In younger children, divorce may reinforce youngsters' implicit memories of criticisms they received from their parents. Any negative implicit memory these children have about themselves also may be affected by disputes between their parents. The kids may suspect that they were the cause of their parents' disagreement.

Some divorcing parents are reluctant to try to explain fully the reasons behind the divorce. Such parents may not believe that the children are mature enough to understand. One parent may refrain from creating a negative impression about the other. By contrast, some spouses look forward to castigating their mates without any consideration of the impact on their children. But a mother may intentionally shield her children from the truth about her mate. Unfortunately, this may leave the kids to speculate that their mother herself might have unreasonably instigated the divorce. Some children, left with believing that dad could do no wrong, unfairly but silently blame their mothers. Children have great imaginations, and what they don't understand they will invent.

Adoption

Adoption from natural parents can reveal some of the most dramatic evidence of implicit memory. Perhaps the place to start is an example of one of the most extreme kinds of cases: adoption of children from Middle European orphanages. Thousands of boys and girls languish for years in these orphanages. Lack of personal mothering can lead to irreparable neurological damage, an inability to socialize appropriately, or to have sexual relations. Because of inadequate funding, conditions are horrible in many of these places:

- Numerous children share each sleeping room.
- Few windows look out on bleak scenes.
- Personal care and nurturing is limited by inadequate staffing and training.
- Food is usually bland and repetitious, and sometimes it is limited.
- Little is available for the abandoned or orphan children to do with their time.
- No effort is made for their intellectual stimulation.
- Time churns relentlessly onward, with no hope that tomorrow will be any better.

Probable language barriers, drastic cultural differences, and the sudden release from "prison" into the warm welcome of an adoptive family pose visible and invisible obstacles for adjustment. In the midst of their silent, uncomfortable awe, such children typically are ill equipped to respond as enthusiastically as the new family anticipates. This may leave the adopting family wondering if they did the right thing. But beneath the perceptible surface of this adoptive occasion lies an accumulation of subtle, unconscious implicit emotions with a long history. Only time will allow these memories to unravel. Some feelings may not show up until the adopted child reaches the age of reason.

The April 2008 *Readers' Digest* contained an article, "Learning to Love." It dramatically exemplified the tribulations of a seven-year-old boy, adopted by American parents from a Romanian orphanage. At first, he seemed to adapt well to his new life. He appeared to love his new world, so different from the first years he spent in the orphanage. There were occasional sleeping problems, a few temper tantrums, and the hurdles of a new language. At one point, he suddenly realized that someone had brought him into the world and then abandoned him. His rage knew no bounds. He was institutionalized several times for treatment, but this fed his anger, and he became intentionally violent.

The boy eventually was diagnosed with "reactive attachment disorder." This is commonly found in abused children, particularly those from orphan adoption mills. Children with this disorder characteristically have a very low self-esteem, with a profound belief that they are "bad, unwanted, worthless, and unlovable." They are unable to love themselves or other people. The result is alienation, reflected in violence and anger. These adoptive parents eventually found an innovative regimen for helping the boy bond with them, slowly but surely. It was a demanding but compassionate effort, and it subsequently was successful.

Adults who know they were adopted typically yearn to find their biological parents, or at least their mothers. One might ask why. Is it to learn the reason for their abandonment? Or is it to fill a heartfelt need to establish a bond they never had with their natural mother? Because implicit memory and associated emotions seem to begin even before birth, perhaps the child senses the failure to bond. Also, if he or she was put up for adoption because of an unanticipated and unavoidable disruption, inevitably he or she may harbor a lingering question of self-worth.

Revelations from Science

As mentioned earlier, neurobiologists reveal that a newborn already has the capacity to feel most of the emotions that adults feel: jealousy, fear, anger, love, and sadness. The infant's implicitly imprinted experiences soon may include the range of emotions that the parents experience and, significantly, that the parents react to. Many times in this book neurobiologists stress the fetus's and the infant's sensitivity to others' states of mind. This remarkable capacity seems facilitated through their receptivity to a wide assortment of interpersonal cues.

As you've also read, an unwanted child eventually is likely *consciously* to realize his undesirable status. Researchers claim that he or she already *implicitly* knows as a fetus! Put yourself in the child's place. Maybe some of you even were there. The potential effects on the child may not be just to mental health but to physical health also. Studies suggest that this can influence not only self-esteem but also social behavior as teenagers and as adults. It doesn't seem a stretch of the imagination to attribute juvenile delinquency and even criminal behavior to such disruptions.

Probably one of the most startling revelations from science is that, despite parents' best-intended, best-informed efforts, their siblings may vary from one another in very individualized ways. There appear to be "outliers, kids who don't turn out the way experts promise." This news was made available in the "Science" section of the August 18–25, 2008, *Newsweek* in an article by Sharon Begley, "But I Did Everything Right!" This is not necessarily a cause for alarm. But it helps put into perspective the influence of an individual's DNA. It also emphasizes the increasing significance of the science of genomics, whereby care of a child can be more targeted to his or her individual makeup.

Personal Comments

This book recognizes, but won't examine, the purported black market in kidnapped or unwanted children. Also, the matters of abortion and contraception persist to be debated widely. For mothers who might abandon or even kill their babies, orphanages exist in many countries. Also, public sites have been identified in this country, to provide a dropping-off point for a newborn and to better ensure attention and care for these babies.

It's very important that the author disavow any appearance of being the new Dr. Benjamin Spock. I'm only, as you may be, a parent of two wonderful adults. Everything you read in this book came from respected professionals in neuroscience, mental health, social science, and child development. I'm just a reporter trying to correlate advances in these fields to share them with you. I doubt that you will be as surprised, even shocked, as I was by what I discovered about the potential impact of implicit and somatic memory on all of us.

In considering the potential impact of such disruptions on human lives, you may wonder if anyone can adapt to facing such pressures without untold lasting negative effects. You may be relieved to hear that such a human capacity does exist. It is called resilience, as you'll discover in the next chapter.

Chapter Thirteen

Resilience: Coping in Today's World

This book focuses on potential problems arising from unforeseeable events facing young children, teenagers, and adults. You may wonder whether there is any hope for improving the outlook for future generations. This chapter examines a quality discovered in some people of being able to cope with almost any disruption in their lives. In the midst of the visible realities that all too often paint a disturbing landscape for people around the world, something truly amazing is possible. Despite all the conceivable pitfalls facing a newcomer, scientists have found some new hope. It rests in their finding that some children, teenagers, and adults are amazingly capable of coping. This has been demonstrated in almost any kind or amount of stress that they encounter. The term "resilient" has been used to describe these people.

Resilience obviously is a physical property that a material object has of withstanding almost any stress and perhaps growing stronger as a result. The tempering of steel comes to mind. It's been said that we may undergo the trials of life in order to grow spiritually. Perhaps resilience is what we should seek for our children. This chapter doesn't imply criticism of parents. Instead, it tries to describe and illustrate this unique capacity some children and adults exhibit to survive and even thrive despite almost any turbulence. In a sense, the present state of society seems to foster uncertainty for newcomers. But please don't attempt artificially to instill resilience in yourself or your children. On the other hand, please don't ignore factors encouraging resilience. These factors simply should make you aware of potentially positive outcomes they seem to encourage in some families, circumstances, and settings.

Origin of the Term "Resilience"

Emmy Werner was one of the first social scientists to use the term "resilience" in her book *The Children of Kauai : A Longitudinal Study From the Prenatal Period to Age Ten.* She led a thirty-year study of 698 infants on the Hawaiian island of Kauai—the island's entire group of births for the year 1955. Underscoring the study was a traditional belief—that children born and reared in dysfunctional family and environmental circumstances are more likely to manifest delinquency, mental and physical health problems, and family instability than children exposed to fewer such risks.

As her study followed the growth of these children into adulthood, the outcome was not as she expected. Surprisingly, many of the high-risk children developed into normal and happy adults. Werner and her colleagues went on to identify several protective factors in the lives of these resilient individuals. These factors seemed to help balance out risk elements during critical periods in these persons' lives. Many researchers appeared surprised by these findings. However, like Werner's study, other research has documented that resilience is indeed a verifiable trait that some people apparently possess.

Recent Research

The article "The Life Course of Psychological Resilience: A Phenomenological Perspective of Deflecting Life's Slings and Arrows" by Norman Watt, et al., was published in 1995 in *The Journal of Primary Prevention.* Watt and his colleagues acknowledged that there is a significant lack of "longitudinal studies of adults who have not only survived extreme early life stresses but have actually thrived in the face of them." Their study involved thirty-one middle-aged adults whom they felt exemplified resiliency despite severe early life adversity. It compared a control group of nineteen adults in comparable life circumstances who were not exposed to such early life stress.

Some researchers caution that offspring, parents, circumstances, and settings are so highly individualized that there is no cure-all guaranteed to succeed. Resilience of individuals may vary in some areas of functioning or in different periods of their lives. Researchers in this field remind us that human nature seems to dwell on the negative. Mental health professionals and the rest of us point to deviant personalities. But we seldom acknowledge the well-adjusted, productive individuals who may or may not have been reared in adversity. We typically count our miseries one by one but let our blessings slip by unnoticed.

An Inherent Trait

A compelling slant to the idea of child resilience was suggested by Barbara Sinor's book *Gifts from the Child within: Self-discovery and Self-recovery through Re-Creation Therapy.* In a sense, there might exist within some individuals an indefinable quality to confront, cope with, and survive even the most stressful circumstances. As a result of what I learned in research for my previous book, I feel compelled to introduce the conceivability of an inner, very personal strength some children appear to manifest. This is best illustrated in Dr. Tobin Hart's book *The Secret Spiritual World of Children: The Breakthrough Discovery that Profoundly Alters Our Conventional View of Children's Mystical Experiences.*

It appears that many variables are involved in achieving resilience—it does not magically appear only in certain children, under specific circumstances, in the presence of only limited trauma, or without the support of others. True to the theme of my book, however, implicit memory invariably would seem to play a significant role in a child's ability to develop resilience. The contribution or detriment of implicit memory to resilience remains indeterminate, of course, due to the relative inability to characterize anyone's implicit mindset.

Contributions to Resilience

Among the factors to which child resilience has been attributed are the following:

- a strong bond with a nonparent caregiver, such as a relative, a babysitter, or a teacher

- a personally rewarding involvement in a church or community group, such as the YMCA;
- a close, trustworthy friend with whom to share mutually both the pleasures and vicissitudes of life;
- a personality that is empathetic, caring, and nurturing of other persons or animals being mistreated;
- a pastime that he or she is passionate about that constitutes a "safe place;"
- a survival attitude, from victim to eventual victor, with a worldview perspective;
- an unsuppressed eagerness or wonder about the miracle and beauty of life as experienced in nature;
- an ability to look beyond the present with anticipation for the future.

The Holocaust as an Example

The Holocaust was probably one of the most publicized group events in which many survivors were applauded as being resilient. Yet these people sometimes were stigmatized; it seemed incomprehensible that they could have survived without some special favor or advantage from their captors. One of the most classical examples of childhood resilience in the Holocaust is captured in psychiatrist Kerry Bluglass's book *Hidden from the Holocaust: Stories of Resilient Children Who Survived and Thrived.*

Another is George Eisen's book, *Children and Play in the Holocaust: Games among the Shadows.* J. J. Sigal expanded on the impact of the Holocaust in his articles "Resilience in Survivors, Their Children, and Their Grandchildren" and "Long-Term Effects of the Holocaust: Empirical Evidence for Resilience in the First, Second, and Third Generation." Atia Daud, Britt af Klinteberg, and Pers-Anders Rydelius also studied the "Resilience and Vulnerability among Refugee Children of Traumatized and Non-traumatized Parents."

Resilience versus Recovery

The subtitle of George Bonnano's article on "Loss, Trauma, and Human Resilience" is "How We Underestimate the Human Capacity to Thrive after Extremely Aversive Events." Bonnano distinguishes between resilience and "recovery." He defines resilience as an "ability to maintain a stable equilibrium." In contrast, recovery is a loss of normal functioning for several months, with full recovery sometimes requiring up to a year or two. This often is characterized by depression or posttraumatic stress disorder (PTSD).

As examples of resilience, he pointed to the death of close friends or relatives as examples of acute distress from which some people bounce back fairly quickly and seem to move on with their lives with relative ease. He apparently felt that the prevalence of resilience is underestimated because these people seldom, if ever, experience psychological problems or seek treatment and therefore may seem rare.

Mental health professionals and clergy long have recommended that people work through bereavement to enable them to handle the emotions and memories about losing a loved one. Not only does empirical evidence fail to support the legitimacy of "working through grief," but it also suggests that this practice may be harmful to some persons.

Some researchers argue that persons exposed to traumatic events may benefit from early psychological intervention, but to impose it on all participants is misguided. Initial screening practices might help identify individuals with risk factors who could benefit. Bonnano feels that many people who experience potentially traumatic events "will show a genuine resilience" which could be "undermined by clinical intervention."

Other Theories

Although some mental health professionals have characterized what may seem to be
emotional avoidance, denial, or delay of grief as pathological, the absence of acute symptoms may actually reflect resilience. "Resilience ... is not rare but relatively common," Bonnano commented. He dismissed the idea that persons exhibiting resilience in the face of bereavement might be cold, unfeeling, or insincere in their attachment. These people showed yearning and emotional loss but this was transient rather than enduring, and the individuals were able to adapt well to the loss.

Some researchers felt that psychological resilience was a trait of unusually healthy people. But recent studies reveal it is more complex, and various factors seem to be involved. A vital question remains as to what commonalities or differences can be found in people's lives possibly to account for their strong coping skills when confronted by trauma.

Bonnano introduced the personality trait of "hardiness" as a source of resilience. This includes ways in which an individual views himself or herself and the world: belief in a worthwhile purpose in life; self-confidence in being able to shape events and outcomes; and belief that life is a composite of positive and negative learning experiences.

Ironically, certain types of resilience seem related to removal of environmental stress. An example uncovered in research involved the death of loved ones when spouses had cared for them as lingering illness gradually diminished the quality of life for both. Surprising to both researchers and participants was the extent of positive coping the survivors demonstrated.

Bonnano identified several types of coping mechanisms. One was "repressive coping," wherein individuals avoid "unpleasant thoughts, emotions, and memories." Such emotional dissociation may be felt to be pathological. This seems to "foster adaptation to extreme adversity." One way repressors and others seem able to cope well with adversity is by expressing positive emotion and laughter. There remains a question as to whether such surface demonstrations are reliable indicators of true resilience. Herein also resides the uncertainty of whether visible representations of positive explicit self-esteem are false characterizations. Only those persons who know the individual well can cut through the visible to the true nature of the individual.

Resilience as Transcendence

In 1993, Robert Jay Lifton published an essay he had prepared in the late 1960s and early 1970s, *The Protean Self: Human Resilience in an Age of Fragmentation,* which met with much criticism. The word Protean refers to Proteus, the Greek sea god who manifests himself in many forms. Lifton's premise was that, in a world of apparent contradiction, we were reared to believe in a reality of "constancy and stability." But we nevertheless face uncertainties and threats to our confidence about our "psychological moorings."

He believed that the human self has demonstrated a remarkable resilience to rise above these challenges and emerge as a victor rather than a victim. Lifton seems to believe that the "essential self" has the innate capacity to see beyond the immediate present and have an unshakable faith in the future of humankind. This self sees beyond a single life's existence to a larger "human connectiveness," which seems to transcend individual incarnations and involve the universe at large. Interestingly, this idea of resilience to trauma does not seem restricted to specific individual backgrounds, but could be related to individuals' psychological and spiritual makeup. The idea of spiritual involvement may be repugnant to some people. But it necessarily includes rare observations of personal fortitude that may seem inconsistent with the population at large.

The Judeo-Christian Bible, 1 Samuel 30:6, reads "But David took strength from the Lord." Pastor Joel Osteen delivered a sermon based on this verse. At that biblical time, David faced an insurrection by his men, following a deadly raid on their city by an enemy group while the Israelis were away. The term "inner strength" has been used to describe people who seem psychologically resilient. Perhaps David's resolve to pursue the invaders and recover his people's possessions and kidnapped families was this sort of inner strength. This does not deny God's involvement, but seems to reinforce the idea that resilience may involve an inner capacity to rally psychological strength from certain convictions, including faith in God.

Liftons's recognition that individuals may vary in their ability to cope with extremes of life may highlight the significance of resilience. There seems to remain a question of whether this involves an adaptation to life's exigencies or an inherent human capacity to rise above worldly challenges.

Family Resilience

Studies have demonstrated that family resilience can differ from individual resilience. James P. Coyle addressed this in his paper "An Exploratory Study of the Nature of Family Resilience." Despite repeated or continuing stress, some families seem to rise above allowing themselves to become dysfunctional. Coyle identified several characteristics that seem to promote family resilience. These include attitude toward the stress and finding ways of resolving it; existence of supportive resources;

and family beliefs, cohesion, communication, and adaptability. Even parent and child self-esteem, cultural pride, spirituality, and high expectations for children were shown to be influential.

Role Modeling

Despite our tacit commitment to serve as role models for others, especially our children, pressures of everyday life often pose obstacles. Even the most devoted role models may forget that their occasional visible behavior may contradict the image they hope to portray, and this may overshadow their most positive efforts. No doubt this sounds like unrealistic idealism. But we have continuing opportunities to exemplify "do as I do, not as I say."

It doesn't seem far-fetched to point to times when very young children are chastised by parents, often with good reason. In the section of this book on nurture, you read that child development researchers stress young children's continuing need for reassurance. You read too that a child's explicit mind doesn't develop until age two to three. His or her ability to understand and reason before that seems limited to registering as authoritative any ultimatum from a parent. Children often are unable to comprehend that criticism or punishment is related only to their behavior at the moment. As a result, they may interpret a parent's censure to mean that they are categorically bad. I think that's why it is recommended that parents balance any such criticism with a comforting reassurance of the parent's continuing love and possibly an explanation for the censure. We are told that the very young often spontaneously exhibit altruism, apparently a sort of empathy. It seems that a parent's demonstration of empathy for a child's feelings about an ultimatum, with reassurance and discussion, could go a long way toward role modeling empathy and helping sustain the child's natural feelings for others.

When role modeling is moved into the arena of older teenagers and adults, there often emerges a variant of human behavior known as hypocrisy. In other words, we seem prone to judge actions by others more harshly than similar actions by ourselves.

A fascinating article by Sharon Begley, "Do as I Say, Not as I Do," appeared in the "On Science" section of the June 23, 2008, *Newsweek*. She revealed how researchers discovered that hypocrisy seems to require a degree of thinking or reasoning. When such higher-order cognitive processes are blocked experimentally, we're left with gut-level or intuitive reactions. Then, we condemn our behavior using the same standards we apply to others.

If you are discouraged by what you have read so far, the next chapter should reassure you. Research continues to uncover promising new vistas for helping us better to understand ourselves and each other. The future looks bright with unfolding opportunities for improving the welfare of humankind.

CHAPTER FOURTEEN

LIGHT AT THE END OF THE TUNNEL

LET'S SWITCH THE PERSPECTIVE FROM fetuses and babies to teenagers and adults. Even though this is almost the end of this book, mental health researchers and practitioners are just beginning to open the textbook of hope—for better understanding of, and positive health benefits from, consciousness, the mind, and the brain. You've heard that implicit behavioral responses are imprinted subconsciously from early gestation through the first few years of life. Also, that the sources of these imprints can be virtually anyone or anything in our surroundings. Then too, our responses to these imprints later in life are both unconscious and unintentional. Hypnotic regression was given as one way to access our subconscious mind and implicit memory. But there are other developments as researchers seek ways to help make these memories more accessible. Obviously, this should improve the treatment of mental illnesses in which the implicit mind is involved.

Mind Chatter versus Meditation

The May 13, 2008, *Oprah Winfrey Show* dealt with past-life hypnotic regression and featured Mehmet Oz and Brian Weiss. Weiss is a prominent Florida psychiatrist who has performed thousands of past-life therapeutic hypnotic regressions. Oz and Weiss emphasized the everyday barrier that "mind chatter" imposes on any efforts to unearth subconscious or implicit memories. They also explained that hypnotic regression simply relaxes the subject's conscious mind and allows him or her to disregard mind chatter. This enables the individual to better access the subconscious mind. They did caution not to expect results on the first try. It may take several sessions.

Some child development researchers even have speculated that children as young as seven years of age soon realize that they can't stop thinking. In other words, "mind chatter" starts very early in life. As onerous as the following may seem, self-reflection, self-consciousness, or meditation have been shown to help. These make implicit imprints more recognizable and more able to be dealt with in daily living.

Benedict Carey helped emphasize the approachability of meditation in his article "Lotus Therapy" in the May 27, 2008, edition of *The New York Times*. Despite the exotic title of his article, Carey provided some very practical information that makes "mindful meditation" seem less formidable. We may intentionally repress explicit memories of traumatic experiences. But mindful meditation seems to slow mind chatter enough to allow some implicit memories to surface consciously. In a sense, it helps provide a bridge between implicit and explicit memory.

Meditation Cautions

Most authorities voice several cautions about meditation. Other conscious thoughts seeking attention will continue to flow and should be allowed to flow. Just don't focus on any of them. Otherwise, they become distractions. The objective is simply to acknowledge memories never recalled previously. Don't attempt to deal with these memories or let them hurt you—simple awareness can be therapeutic. Perhaps most important, try to accept implicit memories in the context in which they were registered: long ago and likely under radically different circumstances for both you and your family. Most experts say that mindful meditation can be a real personal challenge and that it may require several tries before happening. An important reminder: if mindful meditation on your own produces absolutely intolerable memories that you feel compelled to reject, change, or shamefully accept, you should seek counseling from a mental health professional.

Stimulating Insights

In a way, meditation or self-reflection is involved in the idea of focusing on the "now." Ever notice how your mind can wander when you're simply "taking care of business," the daily chores all of us face. Remember the experiences involving procedural memory, mentioned earlier. We may drive past a designated exit or forget to pick up a child at school when our spouses usually do so.

There also are phenomena called "state-dependent," "mood-dependent," and "setting-dependent" memory inducement. In these situations, the implicit memory of a particular event, previously not consciously accessible, may spontaneously pop into your mind. Imagine a time as an infant when you unconsciously felt fear from being left alone and no amount of screaming brought help. Later in life, something unconsciously stimulates that implicit memory. Then you may consciously recall, even though vaguely, that actual experience as a baby. This has been called "making the implicit explicit." State-dependent memory retrieval has been involved in certain kinds of therapy. Rebirthing is one of these. The intent seems to be to encourage a conscious awareness by simulating an event thought to be associated with an implicit, possibly traumatic, memory.

Since the body itself seems capable of registering somatic memory, certain patterns of physical movement or other somatic involvement may induce a conscious revelation. The intent, here again, seems designed to move an experience from implicit memory into explicit memory to be addressed consciously in real time. It seems a sort of transfer from the body to the mind. Other forms of therapy may involve mood-dependent or setting-dependent implicit memory. Certain movements, breathing patterns, gestures, or postures also may be used in therapy. Lesser-intense implicit memories apparently may surface spontaneously as a result of stimuli such as sights, smells, or sounds that seem vaguely familiar.

Moments of Revelation

In his book *Remembering Infancy: Accessing Our Earliest Experiences, Theories of Infant Development,* Alan Fogel defined and recommended recognition of and further research on what he termed "participatory memory." He linked this with implicit memory of early childhood and believes that it offers an opportunity for a "healing change" to occur. Participatory memory is thought to manifest itself in a spontaneous, almost surprising, yet conscious manner. He said that it isn't likely to occur in the press of daily living. It apparently is not retrievable by intent or effort. Yet these events have a "sense of truth" about them. It is as though a memory "comes alive" almost as if someone distinctly relives an experience from his or her distant past, either long forgotten or unconsciously imprinted.

Fogel believes that these apparently vivid recollections occur during periods of intense stress or during certain kinds of therapy, and that these memories have the characteristics of the original experience. The individual may be unable to relate a participatory memory to a specific past time or place. Still, these can have a "transformational" effect that may be therapeutic. He revealed that "now moments" might involve participatory memories. These often are described as part of spiritual or meditative experiences. People and cultures have assigned meaning to these events, such as past-life memories or spiritual insights. Near-death survivors sometimes describe their revelations as "all-knowing" and attribute to them their changed beliefs about life and death.

Participatory memory seems to offer special hope for addressing mental illnesses, especially when linked with new discoveries about our brain's neuroplasticity. This kind of memory has certain characteristics that seem to relate it to state-dependent, mood-dependent, or setting-dependent memory retrieval, in terms of contextual cues or stimuli. Simulation or suggestion should make these useful in mental health counseling. It appears that the intensity of the memory may help account for its life-changing impact. However, there is an apparent paucity of Internet references to the term "participatory memory."

On one hand, you may make these discoveries while you are alone. In contrast, therapists may facilitate these revelations. This allows such memories to be examined in a professional context to achieve the greatest therapeutic benefit. Obviously, if this happens while you are alone, you are left with your own interpretations and capabilities.

Internal Tensions

The potential impact of unrecognized tensions between conscious, intentional behavior and implicit, imprinted responses seems unassailable as one root of mental health problems. Fortunately, most people have learned to deal with such conflicts in a manner that allows them to retain their normal ability to function. At least, this may be how it seems to others. The context of these previously hidden memories need not be threatening or traumatic. They may involve a reassuring situation encountered as an infant, such as a mother's loving smile or warm embrace. But they also may remind us of terrifying events. In both instances, we likely registered a strong emotion, one positive and the other negative.

As an example, I now vividly recall being separated from my mother in a five-and-dime store called Newberry's in Farmville, Virginia, soon after I learned to walk alone. At first, I was fascinated by my surroundings. Suddenly, my mother was nowhere to be seen. I remember my terror. My horrendous screams quickly brought her to my side.

Psychologists might conclude that my experience lingered in my implicit memory and shaped my social interactions even into adulthood. I honestly must admit that I didn't recall that event until much later in life. Also, I'm not certain when or why it spontaneously and consciously reappeared. Furthermore, I still don't understand the specific impact that experience had on my later behavior. But now that I remember it, any terror is gone. For some reason, possibly related, my favorite song over the past few years has been B. B. King's *Stand by Me*.

Other Pathways

Remember that implicit memory seems able to shape our behavior both unconsciously and unintentionally. It therefore seems that consciously recognizing unpleasant childhood impressions or events under the spotlight of the present could help remove some of their sting. Perhaps it also might lessen the full impact of the prior event on our mindset or behavior. Similarly, if we reflectively learn that certain stimuli—people, places, or things—prompt certain feelings or responses within us, this may open our conscious mind to original childhood experiences. We may be able to more effectively deal with their potential impact, especially if the responses happen repeatedly and unintentionally.

Transcendence: The Future

It continues to fascinate me that science and metaphysics seem to share a common bond in the existence of consciousness. One of the frequently reported experiences of near-death survivors and meditation subjects is encountering a "white light," apparently representing a transcendent entity. An Amazon.com reviewer of Deike Begg's book *Rebirthing: Freedom from Your Past,* remarked that "the last third of the book is all about past lives experienced during rebirthing by her clients and contacting the white light."

Jenny Wade noted that a nonphysical transcendent consciousness has been reported at times when the central nervous system is not functioning. She addressed this in her paper "Physically Transcendent Awareness: A Comparison of the Phenomenology of Consciousness before Birth and after Death" in the *Journal of Near-Death Studies.* This appears to occur in the pre-natal state before the central nervous system is fully functioning, and in near-death experiences after the central nervous system has shut down. It is almost as if it pre-dates life and survives death.

Interpersonal Communication

Each of us is bombarded every second by more information than we can handle efficiently. Even in family settings, the assault of time pressures, stress, and constant intrusions by modern technology invade our interpersonal time. These influences suppress intimate interpersonal exchanges. This may be not only a sad commentary on our present state of affairs but also a key detriment to healthy physical and mental development. The development of explicit memory accompanying the acquisition of verbal language and cognition provides major opportunities for interpersonal growth and development of young children. Youngsters seem to thrive on newfound skills of interpersonal communication. Many researchers have emphasized the importance of intimate verbal exchanges to mental health.

Even marriage counselors emphasize this. But daily pressures usually discourage parents from spending personal, uninterrupted time conversing with each other or with their young children. As mentioned earlier in this book, many of us adhere to the rule that "children are to be seen, not heard." Healthy growth and development of a child seems to be a balancing act for both the youngster and his or her parents. A child may seem to be an endless source of attention-seeking behavior. But this is simply his or her wonder-filled exploration of newfound skills of verbal communication, self-controlled physical abilities, and daily discovery of new kinds of experiences.

Narrative

This literally means storytelling. Before the advent of the printed word, traditions and legends were handed down from generation to generation through narrative. Bards used music to make narrative even more attractive to listeners. But narrative also involves the expression of personal feelings and the exchange of such feelings with others. In this context, it has a significant meaning for young children. It helps them not only to make sense of their own minds but also to better understand the minds of others. Ever notice how youngsters never seem to stop talking, even to imaginary playmates if no live person is nearby? Today, we seem to have little time for meaningful interpersonal narrative, except in group settings where we often try to best one another's experiences or achievements.

The earlier belief was that not much meaningful occurs with children in their early years. However, researchers now feel that certain opportunities missed in early years can significantly affect entire lives. Narrative is now one of the most emphasized developmental areas that is inadequately addressed by parents and significant others. This lack may be compounded by parking offspring with non-related, overburdened caregivers, despite the convenience and apparent lack of harm. Fortunately, some youngsters are extroverted enough to compensate for inadequate caregiver-child attention.

One of the chief proponents for the significance of narrative is Daniel Siegel, director of the American Center for Human Development. He is both a pediatrician and a psychiatrist. He believes that explicit memory develops between twelve and twenty-four months of age, as a result of the development of the hippocampus part of the brain. In contrast to implicit memory, this enables a child to become consciously aware of him- or herself. Siegel's ideas are presented in his book *The Developing Mind: How Relationships and the Brain Interact to Shape Who We Are.*

Around the third year of life, Siegel believes, something called "autonoetic consciousness" enables the child to correlate autobiographical recall from explicit memory with other inputs that help make sense of self, others, and the world. One of the inputs that may surreptitiously appear is emotionally charged implicit memories. In effect, narrative may blend explicit memories with certain implicit memories, in an attempt by the brain to "to create a coherent internal interpersonal, family, and community experience." Siegel believes that information transfer across the brain will have occurred sufficiently that, by age four, "children are well able to use words to tell others about their inner feelings and inclinations."

The Dynamic Brain

Science traditionally has held that the brain is organized functionally. In other words, specific senses and individual parts of the body were involved with designated areas of the brain. Also, normally functioning brains were thought to be relatively identical in most people. Likewise, the brain was believed to be most susceptible to growth and development only in the early years of life. People with dysfunctional brains and people whose brains had been injured were thought to have little hope for a normal life.

But a few researchers over many years have positively demonstrated that the brain is dynamic throughout life and their efforts are gaining widespread acceptance. The concept is called "neuroplasticity." The term neuroplasticity obviously means nerve-related, soft, and moldable. But rather than being inert like most plastics, our brains have been shown to continually reorganize themselves throughout our lives. It is not beyond imagination that the brain has "a mind of its own."

Recall that each living cell has been shown to possess an innate intelligence. This enables them to respond to internal and external environmental conditions. Who can dispute the conceivability that brain cells demonstrate this capability through "rewiring?" The billions of neurons nature provides are intended to be an oversupply. In addition to the wiring nature provides through growth and development of the brain, new neural connections continually are formed. These serve to replace, retain, and improve brain functions. Frequently used circuits are strengthened; seldom-used ones may be put to other uses or simply pruned. In fact, while studying monkeys, researchers were surprised to find that the neuronal connections in many brain regions appear to be organized differently each time they are examined!

It appears that rewiring can be stimulated through intentional efforts: in research, in therapy, or even by the brain's own initiative. For example, for a brain-injured child, neuroplastic therapy might involve teaching certain swimming movements. These would encourage his or her brain to facilitate new neural pathways to repair hand-eye coordination. This is called "patterning" and has been used effectively at Johns Hopkins Hospital. Sam Goldstein has even alerted lawyers about this hope for their brain-injured clients, as reviewed in "Neuroplasticity and Traumatic Brain Injury (TBI)" in the Utah Law Injury Weblog.

As mentioned earlier, traditional scientific thinking was that a specific different area of the brain processed each of the five senses. This, too, has been shown to be subject to neuroplasticity. An area deprived of input by acquired blindness may fall into disuse for sight. But the site itself may become rewired to share input from other senses. Alternatively, other sensory sites may be strengthened for their own inputs. It often has been demonstrated that the blind have a much more acute sensitivity to such senses as hearing and touch.

Neuroplasticity now offers hope for literally encouraging the brain to "rewire" itself. Basically, this says that we're never too old for our brains to change. There have been very dramatic examples of patients whose brains and nervous systems have adapted to a variety of disabling neurological conditions. Norman Doidge, a research psychiatrist at Columbia University and the University of Toronto, addressed this in his book *The Brain That Changes Itself: Stories of Personal Triumph From the Frontiers of Brain Science.* He described many cases of neurologically impaired patients who benefited from this characteristic of the brain. His book literally is a biographic history of the researchers who steadfastly held to their findings despite the onslaught of traditional thinking.

But it remains true that the adage "Use it or lose it" is as applicable to the brain as it is to muscles, with regard to our conscious behavior. This seems consistent with the idea that the conscious mind can change the brain. This has been demonstrated in cases of traumatic injury to the brain or to parts of the body, as well as to inborn deficiencies in the central or peripheral nervous systems. Children with dyslexia can be taught to read by stimulating certain movements, improving fine motor coordination. Some eye specialists teach children to enhance their right to left eye movements with eye exercises. Many children improve brain function by playing ping-pong, Frisbee, and other well-designed games. As you read earlier, Michael Merzenich stressed that "brains grow and elaborate and strengthen when they are challenged."

But there also is a dark side to neuroplasticity. Just as conscious efforts to rewire the brain have promise, some undesirable behaviors can become so ingrained that they resist remedial efforts. Established neural pathways seem to strengthen over time. Thus, harmful practices may be perpetuated just as therapeutic efforts can succeed. Ironically, this shows how vulnerable we are to environmental influences and even to how we think.

Jill Bolton Taylor may be the only person I know alive today who has had the opportunity to study the remarkable capability of the human brain from two dimensions of existence. She is a highly trained neuroscientist who, as a brain researcher, suffered a massive hemorrhagic stroke in her left brain. Her eight-year journey to full recovery is magnificently detailed in her book *My Stroke of Insight*.

Stem cells are basic plasticity elements in the brain. Stroke recovery is possible when new neurons grow from stem cells and old neurons that survived sprout new roots and branches.

The Blind Do "See"

Perhaps the most controversial reporting by those who have had out-of-body (OBE) and near-death experiences (NDE) has been their claims of "seeing" from a vantage point distant from their bodies. Witnesses have corroborated descriptions these survivors gave of events that occurred at the time they were "clinically dead." Usually initiated by cardiac arrest, this was manifested by a loss of all vital signs.

In 1989, researchers Kenneth Ring and Sharon Cooper published *Mindsight: Near-Death and Out-of-Body Experiences in the Blind*. An updated edition was published in 2008. Nevertheless, many people still refuse to believe that this could possibly happen.

Skepticism is highly understandable. After all, don't we see with our eyes? So how could even congenitally blind persons possibly "see" during NDEs and OBEs? The pervading belief has been that each of our senses operates using a separate system between the sensing unit and the brain, sometimes called "localizationism." Nothing seems to be further from the truth.

As far back as the 1960s, a four-hundred-electrode contraption was made, resembling a dentist's chair and consisting of "a vibrating back, a tangle of wires, and bulky computers." This is documented in Norman Doidge's book *The Brain That Changes Itself.* Congenitally blind persons sat in the chair with their backs against rows of four hundred vibrating stimulators. In front of the person was a large camera, possibly resembling an early television-scanning device that transmitted signals through a computer. These signals caused different stimulators to vibrate at different times, roughly analogous to the current concept of television pixels. The result was a physically sensed "picture" on the person's back in keeping with light or dark portions of the scene as the camera scanned it. Amazingly, these blind subjects were able to "read, make out faces and shadows, and distinguish which objects were closer and which were farther away." Resolution was poor but was expected to be so. This was called a "tactile-vision device."

Many years later, scientists have tested a modern version using on the tongue a paper-thin silver-dollar-sized sensing device covered with electrodes. This was coupled with modern microcomputers and a small camera attached to the subject's eyeglasses. Brain scans have demonstrated conclusively that the tactile sensations from the tongue are processed in the brain's visual cortex.

Mind-Body Influence

Tied in with the concept of neuroplasticity is the practice of personal reflection. This is the idea of self-consciously asking yourself, honestly, why you are experiencing certain behavior. This is not intended to incriminate oneself or one's parents, but to be useful. Any ancestral pattern of implicit imprints would be noteworthy. Bruce Lipton (2006) claims that our conscious minds can "rewrite subconscious programs" to enable us to rise above limitations imposed by implicit memory. This may be how self-reflection, self-consciousness, and meditation are useful.

One of the most convincing examples I have found of the power of the mind came from the work of Jeffrey Schwartz, research professor of psychiatry at UCLA School of Medicine. His innovative work involved patients with obsessive-compulsive disorder (OCD). It seems that the classic approach for treating OCD had been to make patients confront their fears head-on. In other words, patients who were plagued with believing that everything they touched was contaminating them were immersed, as it were, in their perceived sources of contamination. They were forced to do such things as run their hands around wet toilet seats and handle unwashed dishes. Then they were kept from washing their hands or doing anything else they believed would "cleanse" them. This waiting period lasted until they returned to their pre-exposure level of distress. The underlying theory was that patients' symptoms would eventually "habituate" to this behavior.

Schwartz knew that one cardinal symptom of obsessive-compulsive disorder is something known as an "ego-dystonic" character. This means that, even in patients with severe OCD, some part of their mind acknowledges that their behavior is bizarre. If repeatedly washing hands is the symptom, somewhere in their minds they know that their hands can't be dirty: they just washed them. Their obsessions seemed quite clearly caused by pathological, chemical, or mechanical brain processes. Still, a minor, ineffectual part of them clearly knew what was happening.

Schwartz recognized that the mind's role must have been as an "ineffectual spectator." Each patient was unable to relieve the biochemical imbalances in his or her brain but nevertheless was aware of his or her behavior. Schwartz was thoroughly familiar with what Buddhists call "mindfulness." He had participated in an intensive retreat in the Buddhist practice of mindful meditation. So he concluded that, just perhaps, the "impartial spectator need not remain a bystander." The rest is history.

Schwartz developed a new approach to treating OCD, one that flew in the face of the standard, classical therapy. His success reinforced other researchers' beliefs that the mind is separate from the brain and that the mind can change the brain. This resulted in his and Sharon Begley's book *The Mind and the Brain: Neuroplasticity and the Power of Mental Force.*

Remember, researchers now believe that the mind and the brain are separate entities. Neuroplasticity is the apparent ability of the brain to adapt, heal, repair, and adjust to new circumstances. Basically, this may be facilitated through an effort by the mind—the mind changing the brain. Yes, this seems to be possible at almost any age, not just in the young. Buddhists, for example, are known for their compassion. Some Buddhist monks devote many years, sometimes their entire lives, to meditating on compassion. Some of them consented to being studied with electroencephalographs and magnetic response imaging. It was incontrovertibly shown that the mind could change the brain—not just the reverse, as was previously believed.

Neurobiologists have sought to link specific areas of the brain to memory. They went so far as to train rats to solve a maze, then to remove various parts of their brains. Yet, the rats continued to retain at least some ability to solve the maze. Scientists estimate that the human brain contains nearly one hundred billion neurons. With the multiplicity of connections or synapses between them, there may be trillions of junctions. Meanwhile, the debate continues as to whether our minds—supposedly the sites of memory—are located in our brains. Alternative medicine is increasingly acknowledging that our very thoughts can significantly affect not only our mental health but also our physical health. Two recent books addressing this are John Sarno's *The Divided Mind: The Epidemic of Mindbody Disorders* and Gregg Braden's *The Spontaneous Healing of Belief: Shattering the Paradigm of False Limits.*

Galina Pembroke assembled a remarkable collection of references to illustrate the positive health benefits of one's personal attention to the needs of others. Various terms have been used to designate this state of mind, including love, compassion, empathy, selflessness, and altruism. Her online presentation is "Compassion Rx: The Many Health Benefits of Altruism."

Remember, young children often exhibit spontaneous compassion. This makes us wonder whether lack of attention to others' needs is a learned behavior. If so, what is its goal? The myriad answers may seem so obvious that even the question is redundant. So why focus on helping others? Once we get beyond our personal motives for avoiding attention to others' needs, we may find that we are missing out on a tremendous personal benefit for ourselves.

Pembroke's many citations include such health benefits for those who are compassionate and altruistic as

- suppressing disease activity and activating the immune response,

- healing by decreasing or stopping stress,
- blocking aspects of the stress response,
- alleviating pain, and
- improving longevity and mental health.

The one caution for anyone seeking such benefits is that our bodies can distinguish between mechanical and genuine efforts on our part. As someone quipped, "You can't hide anything from Mother Nature!"

Future of Psychotherapy

Three advances in neurobiology and psychology seem destined to shape mental heath therapy from both the psychotherapeutic and pharmacotherapeutic standpoints. One is the use of new brain imaging techniques. These not only permit longitudinal studies of brain changes over time in the developing child; they also enable researchers to conduct pre- and post-studies of the effects of both counseling and drug therapy. Unfortunately, state-of-research imaging does not yet allow studies to be conducted *during* psychotherapy to determine its impact on the brain.

The second is the recognition of the role of the implicit memory system in mental health. Remember that the implicit memory system unconsciously and unintentionally mediates our interpersonal behavior in response to subtle cues in the environment. Research has shown that this system is fully developed by three to four months of age, stressing the potential influence of the crucial affective relationship between mother and child. Fortunately, new models of psychotherapy promise something like "implicit relearning" to help address this dimension of mental illness.

One promising approach to improving mother-child communication and understanding is called "Filial Therapy." This involves encouraging play sessions at home between mother and child through group training of mothers. Bernard Guerney and Lillian Stover reported on this psychotherapeutic method for treating emotionally disturbed children less than ten years of age. Studies showed significant improvement in the parent-child relationship within six weeks.

The third is the acknowledgment of neuroplasticity virtually throughout life.

It now is recognized that continuing interaction with the environment (as defined earlier in this book) as well as genetics shapes the growth and differentiation of the brain.

Drug therapy may continue to be necessary as a supplement to psychotherapy to help patients manage brief temperamental events like impulsivity and emotional instability. Pharmaceutical research, too, is likely to benefit from these three advances. It is hoped that more targeted pharmacologic agents will be possible to complement other types of therapy.

Advanced scientific techniques now can reveal which parts and pathways of the brain show involvement in certain emotions. The National Institutes of Mental Health described the procedures in their article "Seeing Our Feelings: Imaging Emotion in the Brain." The article reveals that "Scientists have learned to use neuroimaging to see the living, thinking, feeling human brain at work. Neuroimaging tools include functional magnetic resonance imaging (fMRI) and positron emission tomography (PET)." The former uses magnetic fields and radio waves to elicit signals from the brain. The latter uses low doses of a radioactive tracer to obtain signals from the brain.

Both of these technologies have been designed to reveal signals that correlate with human brain activity. These approaches have been used to study the brain pathways involved in sensory processes such as vision and in a variety of cognitive processes. Surprisingly, scientists claim, "We can see that the brain processes information about threat and fear even when the person is not concentrating on it and may not even consciously remember seeing the danger signal."

These tools offer promise, they say. "Although this research still is in its early phase, success to date in delineating specific fear pathways has encouraged the investigations of emotional pathways in mental illness. We are finding out, for example, whether phobias hitchhike on the same pathways used by normal fear. Soon we will have information about other emotions and conditions such as depression. Over time, these tools will be used to study the effects of medications and psychological therapies on mental illness."

Critical Thinking

Perhaps in recognition of the growth of information and the value of disciplined use of mental processes, a concept arose called "critical thinking." It is worth noting for its misuse for self-serving purposes as well as for its intended goal of advancing knowledge for the welfare of humankind. Those persons who pursue selfish interests sometimes refer to the latter practice as "idealistic."

Critical thinking acknowledges the varied mental capabilities of the mind and the brain. It seeks to minimize clutter, waste, and misuse of cognitive processing by thoughtful and reasoned approaches based upon practice and experience. It also realizes that these are simply goals and that all human endeavors are subject to natural limitations. These limitations are imposed by emotion, belief, attitude, mood, and closed-mindedness. The nature of critical thinking therefore may be affected by any underlying motivations.

Critical thinking is the product of a lifelong, self-guided commitment to self-improvement. It is not a simplistic procedure and can suffer from misguided intent, lack of persistence, or lagging devotion. It is the subject of entire books, such as John Chafee's *The Thinker's Way: Eight Steps to a Richer Life* and Karl Albrecht's *Practical Intelligence: The Art and Science of Common Sense*. Standards for critical thinking have been established by such organizations as the National Council for Excellence in Critical Thinking Instruction (http://www.criticalthinking.org/aboutCT/definingCT.cfm).

A Lasting Challenge

Perhaps the biggest hurdle, as I see it, is being able honestly to face the likely fact that our parents reared us as best they thought they could. They unconsciously imparted to us their beliefs about their world and their survival in it. None of this necessarily was malicious. But this confronts us with an untenable personal dilemma. How dare we question our parents' authority or doubt their love for us? Perhaps we might acknowledge the following middle ground.

It may be accepted as personally honorable to respect our childhood imprints as fostered by our family and other ancestors. But the world is in a constant state of flux. Our lives and the lives of others—including our parents—are swept along with it. So we also should feel free to challenge whether our childhood imprints are still applicable in our lives today. Obviously, our implicit imprints are not subject to conscious recall. Yet, as you read earlier, moments of insight may help you identify a self-perceived personal tendency that conceivably could have its roots in your early experiences. These revelations may be the result of personal efforts or the assistance of others. Consider whether these perceptions suggest impediments to a healthy, happy, and successful life. This action alone may fuel your resolve to deal with them in a healthy, energizing manner. Recognize, however, that parents may cling to their own childhood imprints and to the ones they imparted to you. It is understandable that our parents may remain convinced of the validity of their imprints.

This approach should be personally acceptable and emotionally satisfying to us as we mature, so long as we accept this as our personal right and we intend no disrespect for our elders. This, then, should encourage us conscientiously to pursue self-awareness and personal growth as we try to make the world a better place for others and ourselves.

Some ways to pursue personal and spiritual growth are discussed in the following chapter.

Chapter Fifteen

INTROSPECTION

MEDITATION AND PRAYER HAVE BEEN mentioned as examples of ways each of us can "stop the mind chatter" and reflect on our inner selves. Some people understandably would call this a waste of time. Procedural memory and functioning also were discussed. Many of us probably depend on these to survive the increasing crunch of daily living. Remember, this is when we shift our minds into automatic drive in performing our many chores, whether driving, washing clothes, or preparing meals.

Our thinking never stops, of course. Each person's many thoughts are different and some probably race through our heads nonstop. Perhaps the one common denominator we all share is that the substance of our thoughts predominantly has either a negative or a positive nature. We don't need to make excuses for that. It seems to be universal human nature. It is dangerous only when "automatic drive" threatens life or stability. This could happen when we become so disconcerted that we risk an accident—or blurt out a comment we later regret.

You read earlier how some people discipline themselves with critical thinking. You also read about Schwartz's "ineffectual spectator" in cases of obsessive-compulsive disorder. Eckhart Tolle's popular book *A New Earth: Awakening to Your Life's Purpose* seems to have stimulated people around the world to acknowledge their consciousness. The apparent purpose of his book is to promote a realization of how the human mind, if left to its own devices, seeks to satisfy its ego. In a sense, his book seems to introduce an "observer" role.

Basically, being an observer is a natural role as you watch other people: what they say and how they behave. You can almost surmise what they're thinking, whether you're right or wrong. Being an observer of yourself, however, provides the missing element—what you're thinking. Then you can ponder why you behaved or spoke as you did.

Naturally, this sharply contrasts to procedural functioning, acting without thinking. Personal testimonies on the *Oprah Winfrey Show* suggest that Tolle's approach seems to help many persons. The potential effectiveness of the observer role seems akin to Schwartz's success in strengthening OCD patients' resolves to move to a more "effectual spectator" role. The effectiveness of Tolle's views seems undeniable; their persuasiveness may be questionable.

As an example, have you ever represented your work group at a multiday workshop or conference and brought back many ideas for improvement or change? If so, what were the reactions of your colleagues who didn't attend? Skepticism may have prevailed, especially if the recommendations appeared too radical to the status quo. In a similar manner, advocating or adhering to an observer role in shaping conscious behavior may seem like an "uphill battle," whether for others or even just for yourself. It may rebel or go against the grain of our typical upbringing.

Whether you yourself are willing to accept this challenge of introspection or to advocate it for others, one aspect seems paramount. Introspection is most effective when done without distractions, even to the point of disregarding intrusive thoughts. Even though this may seem excessively demanding, an ideal site is your "secret place" or the sanctuary of your own room. Turn off your cell phone, Blackberry, television, iPod, and anything else that makes music, noise, or other interruptions.

You soon should recognize that you're operating in "now" time. Your mind can acknowledge passing thoughts but not dwell on them. Disregard concerns about the past and the future, or at least tell them they'll have to wait until later. Just visit *with* yourself for a time. Think back to your recent behavior. Maybe even keep notes to which you can refer. Honestly examine your feelings at the time. Ask yourself if that's the person you want to be or whether others were controlling you. Tears are natural.

Many times, you probably have talked to yourself, comparing yourself to your friends and your parents to their parents. I bet you think you have it much worse than your friends do. I'm not trying to convince you that you do or you don't.

So, if you've quieted your mind and your surroundings, take these three steps in order. First, admit that you are one of a kind! As someone said, "God don't make no duplicates!" Regardless of how religious or philosophical this sounds, you are unique! No one else has your attributes or your shortcomings. No one but you can excel in your qualities or repair your shortcomings.

Second, convince yourself of the truth in what Brian Weiss said: "Happiness comes from within. It is not dependent on external events or other people." Are there still insistent feelings within you that you don't live up to others' expectations? We become vulnerable and easily hurt when we depend on other people to make us feel worthy, secure, and happy. "Never give your power to anyone else."

Third, try for a minute or two to do what Native Americans suggested: "Walk a moon in the other person's moccasins." In other words, imagine what the world looks like to your family and friends. How might that affect the way your family treats you or how genuine your friends are? What's in it for them? Then try hard for a few moments to stop thinking about yourself and try to understand *you* from everyone else's point of view.

Remember what you read earlier in this book, that each of us has a hidden storehouse of impressions and emotions. This stems from our very early lives and unintentionally shapes our view of the world, other people, and even ourselves. We unconsciously recorded these, and we usually can't consciously recall them. Some may be negative and some may be positive. But times likely have changed a lot since you or I was young. The world and other people have changed too, hopefully for the better. Give yourself and them some credit.

You may wonder whether the insights you have acquired from this book might be turned into a plan for better living. Even as I write this paragraph, I realize that my use of the term "better living" may shift you into a defensive mode. Who am I to suggest that you need to change your life? What right do I have audaciously to prescribe how *anyone* should change? I just stumbled across the book referenced in the next chapter, and I am trying to adopt its wisdom in my own life. So I share it with you.

CHAPTER SIXTEEN

ESSENCE OF LIFE

IF THE INSIGHTS IN THIS book could be distilled into a new view of life, a so-called enlightenment, perhaps no one has offered a better model than Jesuit priest Anthony de Mello in his book *Awareness*. The following were adapted from his book.

- Our emotions control us. Rare is the person who can truly control his or her emotions.
- Our emotions about anything (money, food, power) govern how important that thing is to our life.
- They do not govern how important that "thing" is to our physical existence, although we may believe that it is, but to our ego.
- This means how consciously we are convinced that this "thing" is vital for our happiness.
- For animals and babies, it is security and food.
- As humans grow older, we learn to substitute other "things" that may represent these "necessities," particularly if we become insecure for any reason.
- As babies, we are innocent and immature about life.
- A significant part of our maturation is expected to be our acceptance of requirements that our parents and significant others have for life and for us.

- One of these is that survival demands success in competition with others, and we may succumb to triumphs feeding our ego.

- The most troublesome aspect of growing up is the mirror image we accept of ourselves as reflected by how others treat us.

- We may begin to believe that this image of ourselves is deficient in certain ways.

- So we artificially may try to improve our image by resorting to schemes intended either to comply with what others expect of us or to outshine others.

- All the while, our emotions push us farther away from the innocence we once knew.

- In a sense, we conduct our lives in ways that we believe will satisfy others.

- We are no longer ourselves. We are instruments for satisfying others.

- To regain our true selves and our happiness, we must overcome our role as what has been called an ineffectual spectator.

- This requires us not only to be aware of how we live, but also to take an active role.

- This awareness is strengthened not by our efforts alone but by our willingness to acknowledge the role we typically play as pawns for what we believe other people expect of us.

- This awareness then guides our future happiness, to appreciate life and nature more fully, especially when we are alone with only our innermost selves and when we depend on no one else for anything.

- Then, we enjoy life and other people for the moment, not making requirements of either.

Bibliography

Aamodt, Sandra A. and Sam Wang. *Welcome to Your Brain: Why You Lose Your Car Keys but Never Forget How to Drive and Other Puzzles of Everyday Life.* New York, NY: Bloomsbury USA, 2008.

Adahan, Miriam. 2008. "The Abandoned Baby Syndrome." Chabad. org Society and Living. http://www.chabad.org/library/article _cdo/aid/308404/jewish/Abandoned-Baby-Syndrome.htm

Akhtar, Salman, Selma Kramer, and Henri Parens, Eds. *The Internal Mother: Conceptual and Technical Aspects of Object Constancy.* Northvale, NJ: Jason Aronson, 1996.

Albrecht, Karl. *Practical Intelligence: The Art and Science of Common Sense.* San Francisco, CA: Pfeiffer, 2007.

Amabile, Teresa M. and Leslie A. Perlow. 2002. "Time Pressure and Creativity: Why Time is Not on Your Side." *Harvard Business School Working Knowledge.* http://hbswk.hbs.edu/item/3030 .html

Andreasen, Nancy C. *Brave New Brain: Conquering Mental Illness in the Era of the Genome.* New York, NY: Oxford University Press, 2004.

Aposhyan, Susan M. *Mind-Body Psychotherapy: Principles, Techniques, and Practical Applications.* New York, NY: W. W. Norton & Company, 2004.

Barclay, Laurie and Charles Vega. 2008. "Counseling Interventions Recommended to Promote and Support Breast-Feeding." *Medscape.*

Barrett, L. Feldman, P. M. Niedenthal, and P. Winkielman, Eds. *Emotion and Consciousness,* New York, NY: Guilford Press, 2005.

Begg, Deike. *Rebirthing: Freedom from Your Past: A Revolutionary Way to Change Your Life in 20 Hours.* Hammersmith, London, UK: Thorson's, 1999.

Begley, Sharon. *Train Your Mind, Change Your Brain: How a New Science Reveals Our Extraordinary Potential to Transform Ourselves.* New York, NY: Ballantine Books, 2007.

———. 2008. "Do As I Say, Not As I Do." *Newsweek.*

———. 2008. "But I Did Everything Right." *Newsweek.*

Bluglass, Kerry. *Hidden From the Holocaust: Stories of Resilient Children Who Survived and Thrived.* Westport, CT: Praeger Publishers, 2003. http://ajp.psychiatryonline.org/cgi/content/full/162/8/1553

Bonnano, George A. 2004. "Loss, Trauma, and Human Resilience: How We Underestimate the Human Capacity to Thrive after Extremely Aversive Events." *American Psychologist* 59 (1) 20–28. http://www.nh.gov/safety/divisions/bem/behavhealth/documents/loss_trauma.pdf

Braden, Gregg. *The Spontaneous Healing of Belief: Shattering the Paradigm of False Limits.* Carlsbad, CA: Hay House, 2008.

Brody, Harold and Daralyn Brody. *The Placebo Response: How You Can Release the Body's Inner Pharmacy for Better Health.* New York, NY: Harper Perennial, 2001.

Bureaugard, Mario. *Consciousness, Emotional Self-Regulation, and the Brain.* Philadelphia, PA: John Benjamins Publishing Company, 2004.

Canfield, Jack and Harold C. Wells. *100 Ways to Enhance Self-Concept in the Classroom.* Boston, MA: Allyn and Bacon, 1994.

Caputo, John D. and Michael J. Scanlon. *Augustine and Postmodernism.* Bloomington, IN: Indiana University Press, 2005.

Carey, Benedict. 2007. "Brain Cells, Doing Their Job with Some Neighborly Help." *The New York Times.*

———. 2008. "Lotus Therapy." New York, NY: *The New York Times.* http://www.nytimes.com/2008/05/27/health/research/27budd.html?_r=1&ex=1212552000&en=6e9d0d5b0a0a0724&ei=5070&emc=eta1&oref=slogin

Carver, Joseph M. 2008. "Emotional Memory Management: Positive Control over Your Memory (Part 1)." http://counsellingresource.com/quizzes/emotionalmemory/index.html

CBS, 2006. "What Newborns Are Really Thinking," New York, NY: *The Early Show.*

Centre for Addiction and Mental Health. 2008. http://esciencenews.com/articles/2008/05/01/the.choking.game.psychological.distress.and.bullying

Chafee, John. *The Thinker's Way: Eight Steps to a Richer Life.* Boston, MA: Little, Brown, and Company, 1998.

Chamberlain, David, Ed. 1995. "Prenatal Memory and Learning." *Life before Birth.*

http://www.birthpsychology.com/lifebefore/earlymem.html

Chu, James A. *Rebuilding Shattered Lives: The Responsible Treatment of Post Traumatic and Dissociative Disorders,* Hoboken, NJ: John A. Wiley and Sons, 1998.

"Concepts of the Unconscious." 2008. http://www.psyk.uu.se/hemsidor/staffan.sohlberg/unconsc2.htm

Cosby, Bill and Alvin F. Poussaint. *Come on People: On the Path from Victims to Victors.* Nashville, TN: Thomas Nelson, 2007.

Coyle, James P. 2006. "An Exploratory Study of the Nature of Family Resilience." http://www.csw.ohio-state.edu/phd/docum ents/18COYLE.2.NatureofFROSUS2.pdf

Cozolino, Louis, T. 2007. "The Intrusion of Early Implicit Memory into Adult Consciousness." *Dissociation.*

Curnow, Rick. 2007. "Trauma: A Psychoanalytic Perspective." http://www.aipsych.org.au/articles/aip_trauma_psychoanalytical.pdf

Csikszentmihalyi, Mihaly. *Flow: The Psychology of Optimal Experience.* New York, NY: Harper Collins, 1991.

Daud, Atia, Britt af Klinteberg, and Pers-Anders Rydelius. 2008. "Resilience and Vunerability among Refugee Children of Traumatized and Non-Traumatized Parents." *Child and Adolescent Psychiatry and Mental Health* 2 (7). http://www.capmh.com/content/2/1/7

David, T., K. Goouch, S. Powell, and L. Abbot. 2003. "Young Brains." *Birth to Three Matters: A Review of the Literature.* DfES Research Report Number 444. Nottingham, England: Quees's Printer.

DeHart, Tracy, Brett W. Pelham, and Howard Tennen. 2006. "What Lies Beneath: Parenting Style and Implicit Self-Esteem." *Journal of Experimental Social Psychology* 42, 1–17.

de Mello, Anthony, J. Francis Stroud, Ed. *Awareness.* New York, NY: Doubleday, 1990.

Diamond, Marian and Janet Hopson. *Magic Trees of the Mind: How to Nurture Your Child's Intelligence, Creativity, and Healthy Emotions from Birth through Adolescence.* New York, NY: Plume, 1999.

Doidge, Norman. *The Brain That Changes Itself: Stories of Personal*

Triumph from the Frontiers of Brain Science. New York, NY: Penguin, 2007.

Dougherty, Sarah Belle. 1990. "Mysteries of Prenatal Consciousness." *Sunrise Magazine,* Theosophical University Press. http://www. theosophy-nw.org/theosnw/issues/sx-sbd2.htm

Dreifus, Claudia. 2007. "Through Analysis, Gut Reaction Gains Credibility." New York, NY: *The New York Times.* http://www. nytimes.com/2007/08/28/science/28conv.html

Eisen, George. *Children and Play in the Holocaust: Games among the Shadows,* Amherst, MA: University of Massachusetts Press, 1988.

http://books.google.com/books?id=BUHS3Cx29awC&dq=resilience +children+holocaust&pg=PP1&ots=097KY2AOTr&source=cit ation&sig=X_ZD7D9SPbLYmlkvNFo6CZox4EU&hl=en&pr ev=http://www.google.com/search%3Fhl%3Den%26q%3Dresi lience%2Bchildren%2Bholocaust%26btnG%3DGoogle%2BS earch&sa=X&oi=print&ct=result&cd=1&cad=bottom-3results

Embree, Marlowe. 2008. "Additional Lecture Notes for Unit 6." Marathon County, WI: University of Wisconsin. http://www .marathon.uwc.edu/psychology/360_unit_6b.htm.

———. 2008. "Brief Lecture Notes for Unit 6." http://www .marathon.uwc.edu/psychology/360_unit_6.htm

Emmons, Robert and Michael McCullough. *The Psychology of Gratitude (Series in Affective Science),* New York, NY: Oxford University Press USA, 2004.

Emmons, Robert. *Thanks! How the New Science of Gratitude Can Make You Happier.* Boston, MA: Houghton Mifflin, 2007.

Findeisen, Barbara Reid. 2008. "Life-Long Imprints from Pre-Birth Memories." http://www.childbirthsolutions.com/articles/ pregnancy/lifelong/index.php

Fogel, Allan. *Remembering Infancy: Accessing Our Earliest Experiences,*

Theories of Infant Development, United Kingdom: Blackwell Publishers, 2002.

Frijda, Nico H., Anthony H. R.Manstead, and Sacha Bem, Eds. *Emotions and Beliefs: How Our Feelings Influence Thoughts.* Cambridge, MA, Cambridge University Press, 2000.

Fuchs, Thomas. 2004. "Improving Quality of Care for Bipolar Disorder." *Medscape Family Medicine.* http://bcbsma.medscape .com/viewarticle/493272_1

———. 2004. "Neurobiology and Psychotherapy: An Emerging Dialogue." *Current Opinion in Psychiatry* 17 (6), November.

Gailliot, Matthew T. and Brandon J. Schmeichel. 2006. "Is Implicit Self-Esteem Really Unconscious? Implicit Self-Esteem Eludes Conscious Reflection." *JASNH* 3 (6), pp. 73–83. Reysen Group.

Gardner, Howard. *Creating Minds: An Anatomy of Creativity as Seen through the Lives of Freud, Einstein, Picasso, Stravinsky, Eliot, Graham, and Gandhi.* New York, NY: Basic Books, Harper Collins, 1993.

Gearity, Anne. 2008. "Reactive Attachment Disorder: Mining Gold Using a Child's Map of Attachment." Minnesota Adoption Support and Preservation. http://www.mnasap.org/ information/Factsheets/RADMiningGold.pdf

Goleman, Daniel. *Emotional Intelligence,* New York, NY: Bantam Books, 1995.

Goldstein, Sam. 2008. "Neuroplasticity and Traumatic Brain Injury (TBI)." Utah Law Injury Blog. http://www.utahinjurylawblog. com/2007/06/neuroplasticity_and_traumatic_1.html

Greenwald, Anthony G. and Mahzarin R. Banaji. 1995. "Implicit Social Cognition: Attitudes, Self-Esteem and Stereotypes." *Psychological Review* 102 (1) 4-27. http://faculty.washington .edu/agg/pdf/Greenwald_Banaji_PsychRev_1995.OCR.pdf

Grille, Robin. 2003. "What Your Child Remembers – New

Discoveries about Early Memory and How It Affects Us."
Sydney's Child. Project No-Spank. 14 (4). http://nospank.net/
grille5.htm

Guerney, Bernard G. and Lillian Stover. 1971. "Filial Therapy." MH
18264-01.

Harris, Thomas. *I'm Ok; You're OK.* New York, NY: Avon, 1976.

Hart, Tobin. *The Secret Spiritual World of Children: The Breakthrough
Discovery that Profoundly Alters Our Conventional View of
Children's Mystical Experiences.* Novato, CA: New World
Library, 2003.

Hartman, David and Diane Zimberoff. 2002. "Memory Access to
Our Earliest Influences." *Journal of Heart-Centered Therapies* 5
(2), pp. 3–63. http://www.heartcenteredtherapies.org/go/docs/
Journal%205-2%20Memory.pdf

Hassin, Ran R., James S. Uleman, and John A. Bargh, Eds. *The New
Unconscious (Social Cognition and Social Neuroscience).* New
York, NY: Oxford University Press USA, 2006.

Hepper, P. G. 1996. "Fetal Memory: Does It Exist? What Does It
Do?" Acta Paediatrica Supplement, Vol. 416, pp. 16–20.

———. 2008. "Brainy Babies: Prenatal Stimulation and Brain
Development." *Wellcometrust.* http://www.wellcome.ac.uk/
News/News-archive/Browse-by-date/2000/Features/
WTX024081.htm

Howe, Mark L. and Mary L. Courage. 2004. "Demystifying the
Beginnings of Memory." *Developmental Review* 24: 1–5.

Hunt, Valerie V. *Infinite Mind: Science of the Human Vibrations of
Consciousness.* Malibu, CA: Malibu Publishing, 2000.

James, Leon and Diane Nahl. *Road Rage and Aggressive Driving.*
Amherst, NY: Prometheus Books, 2000.

http://www.amazon.com/Road-Rage-Aggressive-Driving-Steering/

dp/1573928461/ref=sr_1_1?ie=UTF8&s=books&qid=121311112
6&sr=1-1

James, William. *Principles of Psychology.* 1890. http://psychclassics
.yorku.ca/James/Principles/wozniak.htm

Johnson, Cynthia E. 1993. "Children and Competition." North
Carolina Cooperative Extension Service. NC State University.

Kandel, Eric R. *In Search of Memory: The Emergence of a New Science
of Mind,* New York, NY: W. W. Norton & Company, 2006.

http://www2.wwnorton.com/catalog/fall06/032937.htm

Kaye, Bryce. 2008. "Raising Self-Esteem and Reducing Self-
Defeating Shame (Hedonistic Disinhibition)." http://www
.counselingnewbern.com/Staff/BKaye/disinhibition.html

Knight, Kevin. 2008. "Free Will." *New Advent.* http://www
.newadvent.org/cathen/06259a.htm

Krakauer, Jon. *Under the Banner of Heaven: A Story of Violent Faith.*
New York, NY: Anchor, 2004.

Krueger, Charlene, Diane Holditch-Davis, Stephan Quint, and
Anthony DeCasper. 2004. "Recurring Auditory Experience in
the 28- to 34-Week-Old Fetus." *Infant Behavioral Development*
27 (4): 537–543, December.

Lane, Christopher. *Shyness: How Normal Behavior Became a Sickness.*
New Haven, CT: Yale University Press, 2007.

Larson, John and Carol Rodriguez. *Road Rage to Road Wise.*
Ferndale, PA: *Forge Books, 1999. http://www.amazon.com/Road
-Rage-Road-Wise-John-Larson/dp/031289058*

Levinson, Justin D. 2007. "Forgotten Racial Equality: Implicit Bias,
Decisionmaking, and Misremembering." *Duke Law Journal.*
Vol. 57:345, pp.345–424.

Lifton, Robert Jay. *The Protean Self: Human Resilience in an Age of
Fragmentation,* New York, NY, Basic Books, 1993. http://

books.google.com/books?id=R2BlUUQuhN8C&dq=resilienc
e+human&pg=PP1&ots=ymPIRBxB0V&source=citation&sig
=VDwsFROO1bsFEVa3__3eRfY8Dpc&hl=en&prev=http://
www.google.com/search%3Fhl%3Den%26q%3Dresilience%2
Bhuman%26btnG%3DGoogle%2BSearch&sa=X&oi=print&c
t=result&cd=1&cad=bottom-3results#PPP1,M1

Lipton, Bruce H. *The Biology of Belief: Unleashing the Power of Consciousness, Matter, and Miracles.* Santa Rosa, CA: Mountain of Love/Elite Books, 2005.

———. 2006. "The Wisdom of Your Cells." http://www
.brucelipton.com/article/the-wisdom-of-your-cells-part-3

Malone, Thomas Patrick and Patrick Thomas Malone. *The Art of Intimacy.* New York, NY: Simon & Schuster. 1987.

Mancia, Mauro. 2006. "Implicit Memory and Early Unrepressed Unconscious: Their Role in the Therapeutic Process (How the Neurosciences Can Contribute to Psychoanalysis)." *International Journal of Psychoanalysis* 87:83–103.

Massey, Morris. 2008. "Formation of Values and Beliefs."
http://64.233.167.104/search?q=cache:dt0uaJ9faH0J:www
.clairegodwin.co.uk/documents/formation_of_beliefs_notes.pd
f+morris+massey+periods+of+child+development&hl=en&ct=c
lnk&cd=7&gl=us

Masson, Jeffrey Moussaieff and Susan McCarthy. *When Elephants Weep.* New York, NY: Bantam Doubleday Dell, 1995.

Mathews, Michael. 2006. "Freud's Consciousness and the Unconscious." http://www.associatedcontent.com/
article/35396/freuds_consciousness_and_the_unconscious.
html?cat=4

Mayer, John and Peter Salovey. 2008. "All about Emotional Intelligence." http://www.psych.utoronto.ca/users/reingold/
courses/intelligence/cache/about_ei.htm

MedicineNet.com. 2008. "Definition of Implicit Memory." http://www.medterms.com/script/main/art.asp?articlekey=33196

Mendizza, Michael and Joseph Chilton Pearce. *Magical Parent-Magical Child, the Optimum Learning Relationship.* Seattle, WA Midwifery School, In-Joy Publications, 2003.

Merten, Don. 1999. "Enculturation into Secrecy among Junior High School Girls." *Journal of Contemporary Ethnography* Vol. 28, No. 2, 107–137.

Merzenich, Michael. 2008. "On the Brain." Posit Science Corporation. http://merzenich.positscience.com/

Mikulak, Marcia. *The Children of a Bombara Village.* Sante Fe, NM: Sante Fe Research, 1991.

Mines, Stephanie. 2006. "Prenatal Developmental Movement and Parental Response. The Tara Approach Web Log." http://www.selfgrowth.com/articles/Mines1.html

Morse, Melvin. *Where God Lives: The Science of the Paranormal and How Our Brains Are Linked to the Universe.* New York, NY: HarperCollins, 2000.

MSN Encarta. 2008. "Memory (Psychology)." http://encarta.msn.com/encyclopedia_761578303/Memory_(psychology).html.

"New Dads Twice as Likely to Become Depressed, Study Finds." USA TODAY, May 7, 2008.

Nicholson, Jeremy. 2008. "Going with His Gut Bacteria." *Scientific American.*

NIMH. 2005. "Seeing Our Feelings: Imaging Emotion in the Brain" Bethesda, MD, National Institutes of Mental Health. http://www.mental-health-matters.com/articles/article.php?artID=333

Norville, Deborah. *Thank You Power: Making the Science of Gratitude Work for You.* Nashville, TN: Thomas Nelson, 2007.

Oldham, John M., Eric Hollander, and Andrew E. Skodol, Eds. *Impulsivity and Compulsivity.* Arlington, VA: American Psychiatric Publishing, 1996.

O'Regan, Brendan and Caryle Hirschberg. *Spontaneous Remissions Bibliography.* Petaluma, CA: The Institute of Noetic Sciences, 1993.

Paris. Thomas and Eileen Paris. *I'll Never Do to My Kids What My Parents Did to Me.* Philadelphia, PA: Psychology Press, 1994.

Parker-Pope, Tara. 2008. "Better Health, Down on the Farm." *New York Times.*

Parks, Gregory. 2008. "Implicit (Unconscious) Race Bias and the 2008 Presidential Election: Does Obama Stand a Chance?" blackprof.com. http://www.blackprof.com/?p=1966

Peale, Norman Vincent. *The Power of Positive Thinking.* New York, NY: Ballantine Books; Reissue edition, 1996.

Pearce, Joseph Chilton. *Evolution's End.* San Francisco, CA: HarperSanFrancisco, 1991.

———. *The Biology of Transcendence: A Blueprint of the Human Spirit.* Rochester, VT: Park Street Press, 2002.

Pembroke, Galina. 2008. "Compassion Rx: The Many Health Benefits of Altruism." Earthpages.org. http://epages.wordpress.com/2007/10/26/compassion-rx-the-many-health-benefits-of-altruism/

Pert, Candace and S. H. Snyder. 1973. "Opiate Receptor: Demonstration in Nervous Tissue." *Science* 179: 1011–1014.

Peters, Glenn A. 2003. "Fostering the Emotional Development of Your Children." Therapyinla.com

Powell, Andrew. 2004. "Death and Soul Consciousness." http://www.rcpsych.ac.uk/pdf/AndrewPowellDeathandSoulConsciousness.pdf

Prescott, J. W. 1996. "The Origins of Human Love and Violence." *Journal of Prenatal & Perinatal Psychology & Health* 10 (3) 143–188.

Prinz, Jesse J. *Gut Reactions: A Perceptual Theory of Emotion.* New York, NY: Oxford University Press USA, 2006.

Richards, Amy. *Opting In: Having a Child without Losing Yourself.* NewYork, NY: Macmillan, 2008.

Ring, Kenneth and Sharon Cooper. *Mindsight: Near-Death and Out-of-Body Experiences in the Blind.* Bloomington, IN: iUniverse, 2008.

Robinson, Anthony B. 2007. "Articles of Faith: The Unfortunate Age of Entitlement in America." 2007. Seattlepi.com. http://seattlepi.nwsource.com/local/308772_faith24.html

Robinson, Marnia. 2007. "The Brutish Brain." http://www.reuniting.info/science/decrease_of_the_senses_brutish_brain

Rohner, R. P. and A. Khaleque. 2002. "Parental Acceptance-Rejection and Life-Span Development: A Universal Perspective." *Online Readings in Psychology and Culture* 11: 4, http://www.ac.wwu.edu/~culture/Rohner_Khaleque.htm

Ruggles, Tammy. 2008. "Gift from Within: The Resilient Child." http://www.giftfromwithin.org/html/reschild.html

Russo, Nancy Felipe, Henry P. David. 2002. "When Pregnancies Are Unwanted." *Psychology and Reproductive Choice,* The Society for the Psychology of Women. http://www.prochoiceforum.org.uk/psy_ocr2.asp

Rustin, Judith and Christina Sekaer. 2004. "From Neuroscience of Memory to Psychoanalytic Interaction: Clinical Implications." *Psychoanalytic Psychology* 21:70–82. http://www.pep-web.org/document.php?id=ppsy.021.0070a

Sandler, Joseph. *Freud's Models of the Mind.* London, England: Karnac Books, 1997.

Sarno, John E. *The Divided Mind: The Epidemic of Mindbody Disorders*. New York, NY: Harper Paperbacks, 2007.

Schore, Allan N. "The Experience-Dependent Maturation of a Regulatory System in the Orbital Prefrontal Cortex and the Origin of Developmental Psychopathology." *Development and Psychopathology* 8: 55–87.

Schwartz, Gary, William L. Simon, and Richard Carmona. *The Energy Healing Experiments: Science Reveals Our Natural Power to Heal*, New, NY: Atria, 2007.

Schwartz, Jeffrey M., and Sharon Begley. *The Mind and the Brain: Neuroplasticity and the Power of Mental Force*. New York, NY: HarperCollins, 2002.

Sheldrake, Rupert. *The Hypothesis of a New Science of Life: Morphic Resonance*. Rochester, VT: Park Street Press, 1981.

Siegel, Daniel J. *The Developing Mind: How Relationships and the Brain Interact to Shape Who We Are*. New York, NY: Guilford Press, 1999.

Siegel, Daniel and Mary Hartzell. *Parenting From the Inside Out*. New York, NY: Tarcher, 2004.

Sigal, J. J. 1995. "Resilience in Survivors, Their Children, and Their Grandchildren." *Echoes of the Holocaust*: 4. http://www .holocaustechoes.com/4sigal.html

———. 1998. "Long-Term Effects of the Holocaust: Empirical Evidence for Resilience in the First, Second, and Third Generation." *Psychoanalytic Review* 85: 579-585. http://www .pep-web.org/document.php?id=psar.085.0579a

Sinor, Barbara. *Gifts from the Child within: Self-discovery and Self-recovery through Re-Creation Therapy*. Ann Arbor, MI: Loving Healing Press, 2007.

Solomon, Robert. *Not Passion's Slave: Emotions and Choice*. New York, NY: Oxford University Press USA, 2003.

————. *True to Our Feelings: What Our Emotions Are Really Telling Us.* New York, NY: Oxford University Press USA, 2006.

"Some Key Reiki Concepts." WebHealthCenter.com. 2000. http://www.webhealthcentre.com/altmed/reiki/concept.asp

Spencer, Steven J., Steven Fein, Mark P. Zanna, and James M.Olson. Eds. 2003. "The Study of the Psychological Unconscious: From Implicit (Social) Cognition to the Implicit Self-Concept." *Motivated Social Perception*, Mahwah, NJ: Lawrence Erlbaum Associates.

Srivastava, Pramod K. 2008. "New Jobs for Ancient Chaperones." *Scientific American.* 299: 1.

Stephens, Laura. 2006. "Narcissistic Personality Disorder." *Psychology Today.* http://psychologytoday.com/conditions/narcissistic.html

Strachey, James, Ed. *Sigmund Freud: Collected Papers, Volume 5.* New York, NY: Basic Books, 1959.

Tafarodi, Romin W. and Caroline Ho. 2006. "Implicit and Explicit Self-Esteem: What Are We Measuring?" *Canadian Psychology* 47 (3) 193–202.

Tannen, Deborah. 1998. "For Argument's Sake: Why Do We Feel So Compelled to Fight about Everything?" The Washington Post. http://www.georgetown.edu/tannen/argsake.htm

Taylor, Edward W. 1997. "Implicit Memory and Transformative Learning Theory: Unconscious Cognition." *1997 AERC Proceedings.* http://www.edst.educ.ubc.ca/aerc/1997/97taylor1.htm

Taylor, Jill Bolton. *My Stroke of Insight.* New York, NY: Viking Penguin, 2008.

"Teenager Self Esteem: Developmental Periods." 2008. *Internet-of-the-Mind.* http://www.internet-of-the-mind.com/teenager_self_esteem.html

"The Brain From Top to Bottom: The Amygdala and Its Allies." The Canadian Institutes of Health Research and the Canadian Institute of Neurosciences, Mental Health, and Addiction http://thebrain.mcgill.ca/flash/a/a_04/a_04_cr/a_04_cr_peu/a_04_cr_peu.html

Thomas, Nigel J. T. 2008. "Imagination, Mental Imagery, Consciousness, and Cognition: Scientific, Philosophical and Historical Approaches." http://www.imagery-imagination.com/

Timpke, Kevin. 2006. "Free Will." *The Internet Encyclopedia of Philosophy.*

http://www.iep.utm.edu/f/freewill.htm

Tolle, Eckhart. *A New Earth: Awakening to Your Life's Purpose.* London, England: Penguin Books, 2006.

Twenge, Jean M. *Generation Me: Why Today's Young Americans Are More Confident, Assertive, Entitled—and More Miserable Than Ever Before.* New York, NY: Simon & Schuster, 2006.

Wade, Jenny. 1998. "The Phenomenology of Near-Death Consciousness in Past-Life Regression Therapy: A Pilot Study." *Journal of Near-Death Studies* 17 (1).

———. 1998. "Physically Transcendent Awareness: A Comparison of the Phenomenology of Consciousness before Birth and after Death." *Journal of Near-Death Studies* 16 (4).

Watt, Norman F., James P. David, Kevin L. Ladd, and Susan Shamos. 1995. "A Phenomenological Perspective of Deflecting Life's Slings and Arrows." *The Journal of Primary Prevention* 15 (3). http://www.springerlink.com/content/b28t634284k56240/

Weber, Elke and Eric Johnson. "Constructing Preferences from Memory." https://vlab2.gsb.columbia.edu/decisionsciences.columbia.edu/uploads/File/Articles/PAM.slovicbookclean.pdf

Wegner, Daniel M. *The Illusion of Conscious Will.* Cambridge, MA:

MIT Press, 2003. http://www.amazon.com/Illusion
-Conscious-Will-Bradford-Books/dp/026273162

Weiss, Brian. *Messages from the Masters: Tapping Into the Power of
Love.* New York, NY: Warner Books, 2000.

Werner, E. E. *The Children of Kauai : A Longitudinal Study from the
Prenatal Period to Age Ten.* Honolulu: University of Hawaii
Press, 1971.

Wikipedia. 2008. "Imagination." http://en.wikipedia.org/wiki/
Imagination

Wilson, Timothy D. *Strangers to Ourselves: Discovering the Adaptive
Unconscious,* New York, NY: Belknap Press, 2004.

Winter, P. Anne. 2000. "Eternal Moments." *Survivorship*, IX (3).

Yabroff, Jennie. 2008. "The Feminine Mistakes." *Newsweek.*
Yen, Duen Hsi. 1997. "Shame." http://www.noogenesis.com/malama/
shame.html

INDEX

A
Aamodt, Sandra A., 75
abandonment, 106
abuse, 106–107
adolescence
  brain development in, 86
  choking game, 38–39
  entitlement, 63–65
  immature inhibition in, 40
  secrecy in, 42
  self-esteem in, 57–58, 63–64
  societal influence in, 13
adoption, 93, 96–97, 110–111
advertising, 12, 40–41
affect, 24
af Klinteberg, Britt, 116
aggression, 67–69
Akhtar, Salman, 94
Albrecht, Karl, 137
alcoholism and addiction, 15,
  63, 98, 108
altruism, 62, 120, 134–135
Alzheimer's disease, 7, 101
Amabile, Teresa M., 44
American Academy of Pediatrics,
  36

American Center for Human
  Development, 128
amygdalae, 23, 76, 82
"An Exploratory Study of
  the Nature of Family
  Resilience" (Coyle),
  119–120
Annals of Internal Medicine,
  35–36
Aposhyan, Susan, 102
arguments, 68, 79
"Articles of Faith: The
  Unfortunate Age of
  Entitlement in America"
  (Robinson), 64
attachment, 96, 99
attention, 28
attunement, 97–98
Augustine and Postmodernism
  (Caputo and Scanlon), 4
auras, 88
autobiographical memory. *See*
  explicit memory
Awareness (de Mello), 142–143

161

Buddhist monks, 17, 133–134
Bureaugard, Mario, 76
"But I Did Everything Right" (Begley), 112

C
Canadian Institute of Neurosciences, Mental Health, and Addiction, 23
Canadian Institutes of Health Research, 23
Canfield, Jack, 58
Caputo, John D., 4
Carey, Benedict, 82–83, 123
Chafee, John, 137
chakras, 88
Chamberlain, David, 92
child abandonment, 106
child abuse, 24–25, 106–107
child development
    abuse and trauma during, 23, 24–25, 106–111
    of fetus and newborn, 22, 33, 73–74, 82–85, 91–96, 111
    interpersonal communications and, 127–128
    play, importance of, 42, 60, 101
    See also adolescence
Children and Play in the Holocaust: Games among the Shadows (Eisen), 116
The Children of a Bombara Village (Mikulak), 39
The Children of Kauai: A

Longitudinal Study from the Prenatal Period to Age Ten (Werner), 114
choices, making, 20–21
choking game, 38–39
cognition, 24, 55
Come on People: On the Path from Victims to Victors (Cosby and Poussaint), 3
commercialism, 12, 40–41
compassion, 62, 120, 134–135
"Compassion Rx: The Many Health Benefits of Altruism" (Pembroke), 134–135
competition, 59–61
compulsivity, 78
conation, 24
conscious memory. *See* explicit memory
conscious mind, 24, 26–27, 46, 130
consciousness, 2, 26, 29, 127, 139
Consciousness, Emotional Self-Regulation, and the Brain (Bureaugard), 76
conscious universe, 29
"Constructing Preferences from Memory" (Weber and Johnson), 20
Cooper, Sharon, 131
Cosby, Bill, 3
"Counseling Interventions Recommended to Promote and Support Breast-Feeding" (Barclay and Vega), 35–36